Vegan
BURGERS AND BURRITOS

Vegan
BURGERS AND BURRITOS

EASY AND DELICIOUS WHOLE FOOD RECIPES FOR THE EVERYDAY COOK

Sophia DeSantis
FOUNDER OF VEGGIES DON'T BITE

PAGE
PAGE STREET
PUBLISHING CO.

PAGE STREET
PUBLISHING CO.

First published in 2017 by

Page Street Publishing Co.

27 Congress Street, Suite 105

Salem, MA 01970

www.pagestreetpublishing.com

Distributed by Macmillan, sales in Canada by The Canadian Manda Group.

21 20 19 18   2 3 4 5

ISBN-13: 978-1-62414-479-0

ISBN-10: 1-62414-479-9

Library of Congress Control Number: 2017906783

Cover and book design by Page Street Publishing Co.

Photography by Sophia DeSantis. Lifestyle photography by Chris Nelson, Chris Nelson Photography.

Printed and bound in China

There are so many people I could dedicate this book to . . . My village meant the world to me throughout this entire process. But on April 19, 2017, after a rough, emotional day, I opened my laptop and the peace and clarity came to me.

I finish this book just like it began: for my sister-in-law Christine, the first person to try my very first recipe when this book idea was a tiny seed. She looked at me and said, "You nailed this one." Her strength and drive to beat cancer was beyond words. And although she's not here to see this book's completion, I know she's here with us in spirit. May you be eating many burritos in heaven, sweet sister.

Burgers

Burritos 75

Sauces 129

Sides  169

Introduction

Me. The real deal.

The fact that I am writing an intro in a real book is mind-blowing to me. Like, people are actually going to see my name in print. Not just on a silly little blog, but on a book. One that is sold in big places like Amazon. I want to jump with excitement and throw up from nervousness all at once.

This was no easy task. Being a mom to three kids, currently ranging from two to six years old, having a husband who travels for work and managing life overall, let alone keeping up with a blog and "on the side" writing this book, was something short of a miracle. I am not going to say it was smooth, because there were meltdowns, by all of us. Even as I sit here typing, I am being yelled at by the two-year-old about why his avocado is inside the burrito. God forbid. I stop what I'm doing to remove said avocado, only to spark another tantrum as to why his burrito does not have avocado. This is me. This is my life. And as crazy as it is, I love it. I am not a supermom. I am simply like every other mom out there trying to make life work. And what works is different for all of us. Creating recipes, photographing them and sharing them with others is something I enjoy. And when I don't, I don't do it. But mostly, it's a way for me to get my creativity out. I have always been the creative type, and that has taken many forms over the years. Now it's through food, but who knows where life will go from here.

Other than forcing my family to eat my wild creations, I love to play with my kids, exercise, go on date nights with my husband, drink wine, eat good food and spend time with my friends. My ultimate life goal is balance. As much as I love my kids, I also love myself. I simply cannot be the best mom and wife possible if I don't take care of me. This book is the perfect example of that. I did this book for me. Because it was a lifelong dream that felt right when the opportunity fell in my lap. I will be the first to admit that my kids didn't have the best mom, nor did my husband have the best wife, these last couple of months that I have been fully focused on this project. But I personally believe that it's okay. It's good for them to see me do something for me, especially something as big as writing a book. It wasn't forever and now that I am done, they get center stage again. I am proud of the end result, and I hope that one day when my kids grow up, they can understand how big this was and perhaps think something other than, "When are we going to have something for dinner besides burgers and burritos?"

To every one of you reading this, thank you. Thank you for your support, and I hope that you will find some favorites in this large collection of our favorites. Please feel free to reach out anytime with questions! I am truly blessed to have had this opportunity to share my love of food with all of you!

Sophia T DeSantis

WHY MOSTLY PLANTS?

November 2012. That's when we decided to try this silly little 21-day elimination diet to see how my husband felt with no animal products in his body. I thought he was crazy, but he wanted to feel good again. After being told by multiple doctors that his high blood pressure and high cholesterol were genetic and that he would simply need to take medication, he met a cardiologist who said something different. Three months into our new mostly plant-based eating, he was no longer on medication and was doing incredible. One year later, my blog, Veggies Don't Bite, was born. Our lives were changed forever, we felt amazing and my husband's health was more than great. We decided it was time for a change: this was how our family would move forward. So here we are, much sooner than I expected, with a book to give the world some delicious, satisfying and sometimes wild, sometimes simple recipes that just so happen to be free of meat, dairy and eggs. All whole foods and all fairly easy-to-find ingredients.

People make changes for many reasons. Ours was for health, for keeping my husband feeling good on a day-to-day basis and keeping him alive. Why did we all change? Because we are a family. We are in this life together, the good, the bad and the ugly. And the truth is, my boys are all part him, so the chance that they too have the same issues is pretty high. Me, well, I am in this for support. To show love in a different way. Could I eat what I want when I'm not around him? Well, yes, totally. But in all honesty, I don't miss meat. Right before we changed our diet, I was pregnant with our second son, and meat repulsed me during my pregnancy. I couldn't eat it at all, and even the smell sent me to the trash can. Puke city to say the least. So this change wasn't a huge jump for me. And I feel amazing! I ran my first three half marathons within the first ten months of our new diet with no problems, and got some pretty fast times to boot. My primary care doctor is a plant-based eater herself, so if I ever have issues, she is there for support and has true knowledge of all things medical as related to vegan eating. And so far, we are all doing great.

All that being said, we also live a life of balance. In our home, we are able to control what we make, buy and eat. But out in the world, there are many variables. Which is why we have made a conscious choice to let a lot go. This isn't what works for everyone, but when we think about our reasons for change, our health, we believe that balance plays a key role in that. For us, trying to control everything at once causes a lot of stress. Stress is a huge factor when it comes to health and can easily counteract any benefits of eating well. We want to raise our kids to have a healthy relationship with food, and we believe part of that is knowing that it's okay to let it go sometimes. Our kids eat ice cream and cake at birthday parties, they eat candy on Halloween, and when we go out to eat, we don't worry if our veggie burgers have eggs or if the fries are cooked in the same fryer as the chicken nuggets. This is simply how we are able to maintain a happy and healthy life, which is the number one priority for us and our children. The truth is there is no "food police," as much as others try to impose that idea on you. There is no magic diet, no magic way to live your life. We are all different and finding that perfect balance is a gift.

Why burgers and burritos with a heavy helping of sauce? Why **not** burgers and burritos! And sauce is the frosting on the cake, the chocolate chips on the cookie. A plant-based diet does not mean eating only salads. Salad is an appetizer to me. If it's going to be my main meal, then it better have loads of toppings and a dressing I can bathe in. In fact, just give me a tortilla to wrap around said salad, and then I will be satisfied to the core.

Food needs to get me excited. The mother of all meals is full of nutrients but also satisfies me from the inside out, like being in a cozy blanket on a comfy couch. The unicorn of recipes is what I am trying to deliver here— 75 unicorns to be exact. And when I think about unicorns, I come back to patties in a bun or things wrapped in a tortilla. All smothered in sauce. And, yes, all sauces you can eat with a spoon.

Everything in this book is a peek into our daily life. For real, have you seen the photo of me trying to cook a burger while my family is a circus show around me? That is my life. Every. Single. Day. I have mastered the art of dodging children while in the kitchen. And as I do so, I focus on creating flavorful, delicious recipes made with whole foods. This is not to say that we never indulge in processed crap; we do on occasion; remember my talk on balance? But mostly, we can easily satisfy ourselves, and the ridiculous appetites of our three monsters, with whole foods.

Which led me to create this book full of easy-to-find ingredients thrown together into mostly easy recipes, and often devoured by all. Sometimes one kid decides today is the day he refuses to eat anything round. Sometimes meals end up on the floor. But most often, and perhaps after a peek at the dessert the kids won't have if they don't eat their dinner (because if you're not hungry for dinner, then you obviously are way too full for dessert), the food is consumed in utter silence.

Sometimes the kids' meal looks just like ours, and other times I use the same meal and present it in a little more kid-friendly way. Burgers become nugget-size, with fixings on the side. Burritos sometimes become bowls. And sauces may become soup; hey, I don't blame the two-year-old here. But the food remains the same: wholesome, delicious and satisfying.

THE BASICS

We all need to start somewhere.

The two tools that I cannot live without are my food processor and my Vitamix (but any high-speed blender is great). With these and a few other basic kitchen tools, you can easily create everything in this book.

If you don't have a food processor, you can use a blender to slowly chop and combine ingredients. You can also use a knife to chop ingredients a little more finely than normal and your hands to mush up beans. A food processor, though, will give you the best end result.

My Vitamix is used for many cashew-based sauces I make and gives an amazing end result without leaving chunky cashew pieces. But if you aren't an owner of a high-quality high-speed blender, you still have work-arounds. I go over these in the recipes themselves, but you can use any of these great options in place of a high-speed blender:

- Soak the cashews overnight, or for at least 2 hours.
- Boil the cashews for 30 minutes.
- Use a coffee grinder to grind the cashews into a fine powder.

MANAGING YOUR BURGERS

All of the burger recipes make between four and five burgers, depending on how big you like them. To me, veggie burgers can't be thin, weak little patties. They are filled with power-packed ingredients, so the more you can pack into one patty, the better! I make them wide enough to fit a bun and about ¾-inch (2-cm) thick. But by all means, make them how you like them, because life is too short not to follow your belly. Just make sure to adjust the cooking time.

As with many things, these burger mixtures are best when set aside for a while for the flavors to get fully absorbed. It also helps the texture for the moisture-sucking ingredients (like cornmeal, oats and rice) to have time to absorb and balance the moisture. So letting mixtures sit for at least 20 minutes, or even overnight, helps bring out the true flavors.

How you cook your burgers ultimately comes down to preference. I give suggestions in each recipe and will let you know if the burger is delicate and perhaps better when baked than when grilled, but overall it's up to you. Most of the time, I cook burgers in a pan on the stovetop over medium heat for 15 minutes on each side. Pans and stovetops vary, so begin to check the burgers at 10 minutes. If you try to slide your spatula under a patty and it won't give, then it isn't ready and needs to cook longer. If you don't use a nonstick pan, then you may want to prepare the pan by brushing it with a tad of oil to avoid sticking. You can also bake the burgers on a parchment-lined cookie sheet at 375°F (191°C) for about 20 to 25 minutes on each side. Allow burgers to cool and set for at least 5 to 7 minutes to get the best out of the structure and texture.

BECOMING A BURRITO MASTER

Rolling burritos gets easier with practice. I'm not going to lie—I've pretty much mastered it. Let me teach you my ways, young grasshopper.

1. Place ingredients in the center of the tortilla. Make sure not to overfill (don't ask me how many times I've made this mistake).

2. Fold the bottom of the tortilla up to cover the ingredients.

3. Fold the left and right sides toward the center.

4. With both hands on top of the tortilla, almost cupping the ingredients underneath, roll once (almost like you are flipping that section over).

5. Fold the sides (two wing-like sections) inward and tuck them under the ingredient pocket.

6. Using both hands again, cup the burrito and firm up the tightness of the ingredient pocket. Then roll one more time to the end of the tortilla.

I love to grill all of my burritos on the stovetop over medium heat for extra crispy texture. I start with the seam side down, about 5 to 8 minutes on each side, depending on how crisp I want them. For kids, five minutes on the seam side is plenty to seal the seam so that they can eat their burritos without frustration. I also bake some of the burritos in this book. Mixing it up is a great way to keep things exciting; your kids may actually behave during dinner.

LEVELS OF RECIPE MASTERY

Level I: Help! Where's the kitchen? This recipe is for the beginner. As long as you can hold a knife, operate a button and measure correctly, you are golden.

Level II: I can cook. This recipe may need a little forethought but is still fairly simple. Read ahead to make sure you're prepared for a few extra steps.

Level III: I'm not scared of getting fancy. This recipe requires some skill. Whether it's managing more than two parts at once or needing to judge when something looks done, you may want to make sure your kids are kept busy so you can focus.

For more information, check out "Help! I Screwed It Up (and Other Resources)" on page 178.

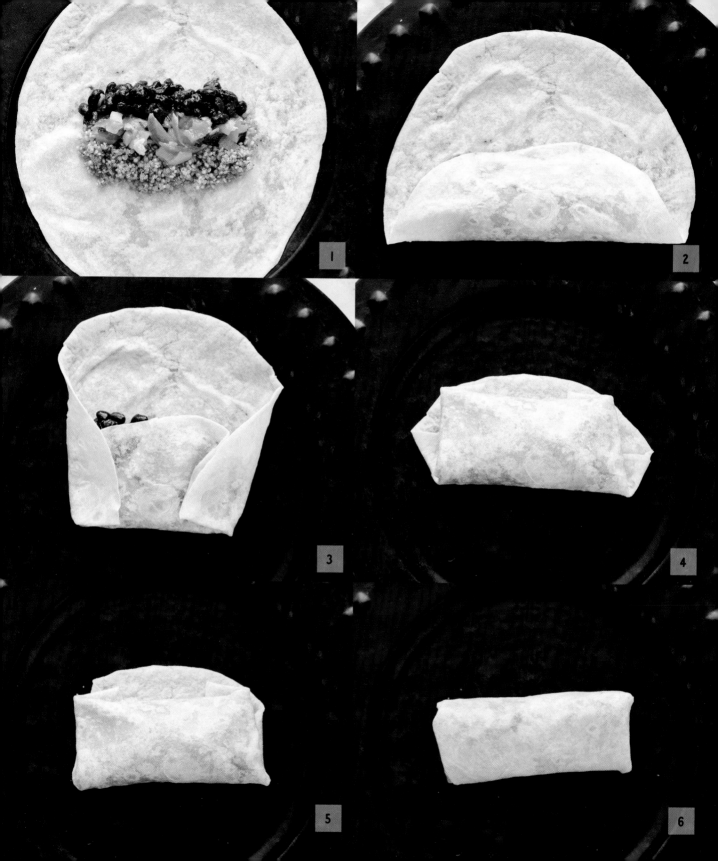

Burgers

My name is Sophia, and I am a veggie burger snob. There is nothing worse than a sad, limp, mushy, unflavored burger. I started creating my own veggie burgers way before we stopped eating meat. Even then, I was always drawn to the flavor and creativity veggie burgers could bring, but the options in the store were miserable.

Even before restaurants began making their own varieties, my kitchen became a burger laboratory. I tested burgers using any and all ingredients from primarily veggie filled to bean based. My obsession was real. The possibilities are endless, and I'm here to show you the possibilities are delicious. Now I throw together ingredients like no one's business, all while dodging a kid or two and flipping dinner for a family of five burger addicts.

BREAKFAST "SAUSAGE" PATTIES

Breakfast just went to a whole new level with these easy-to-prep-and-store breakfast patties. When that savory breakfast craving hits, heat one of these up, snuggle it between two English muffin slices, add your favorite toppings and devour. All the protein you need to start the day right, because sometimes we get sick of smoothies.

1½ cups (302 g) cooked or canned chickpeas, drained and rinsed (reserve the liquid)

3 tbsp (45 ml) liquid from the can of chickpeas (see notes)

¼ cup (40 g) steel-cut oats (gluten-free if needed)

1 tbsp (10 g) potato starch (not potato flour)

2 tsp (10 ml) fresh lemon juice

2 tsp (1 g) dried oregano

1 tsp sea salt

1 tsp dried thyme

1 tsp red pepper flakes

½ tsp ground black pepper

½ tsp crushed fennel (see notes)

¼ tsp dried sage

TO SERVE

4 to 5 English muffins

Tomato slices

Avocado

Healthy Vegan Mayo, WHAT? (page 147)

Put the chickpeas, chickpea liquid, oats, potato starch, lemon juice, oregano, salt, thyme, red pepper flakes, black pepper, fennel and sage in a food processor, and pulse to incorporate. Pulse again slowly, and do not overmix. You want the mixture chunky but crumbly, not like hummus.

Place the mixture into a bowl, and put it in the fridge for at least 20 minutes; an hour is best. Making this the day before and letting it sit overnight is optimal. This helps all the flavors marinate and leads to a sturdier burger.

To cook, shape the mixture into patties. If you're not using a nonstick pan, then you may want to prepare the pan by brushing it with a tad of oil to avoid sticking. Place the patties in a pan on the stovetop over medium heat for 15 minutes per side. Pans and stovetops vary, so begin to check the patties at 10 minutes. If you try to slide your spatula under a patty and it won't give, then it isn't ready and needs to cook longer.

You can also bake the patties on a parchment-lined cookie sheet at 375°F (191°C) for about 20 to 25 minutes on each side. Allow the patties to cool and set for 5 to 7 minutes.

Serve on an English muffin with the toppings of your choice.

Notes: The liquid from the can of chickpeas is also known as aquafaba. It is a binder that helps keep the patties together. I reserve extra and freeze it in ice cube trays for future use.

For the crushed fennel, I simply take regular dried fennel seed and crush it with the back of a spoon. This helps disperse the flavor better throughout the burgers.

Kids: Make patties into a smaller slider size or into nuggets. Serve mayo on the side as a dipper.

APPLE SAGE "SAUSAGE" BURGER

A twist on the traditional breakfast patty, this breakfast burger has loads of flavor without the saturated fat and processed ingredients. Greasy sausage no more, this whole food brekkie keeps me full and satisfied as I go about my day, and Lord knows I need the energy.

1½ cups (300 g) cooked or canned chickpeas, drained and rinsed (reserve the liquid)

3 tbsp (45 ml) liquid from the can of chickpeas (see notes)

¼ cup (40 g) steel-cut oats (gluten-free if needed)

1 tbsp (10 g) potato starch (not potato flour)

1 tbsp (2.5 g) chopped fresh sage leaves

1 tsp sea salt

½ tsp ground black pepper

½ tsp crushed fennel (see notes)

¼ tsp garlic powder

⅛ tsp allspice

½ cup (90 g) chopped peeled apples (I prefer a tart variety)

TO SERVE

4 to 5 rolls

Arugula

Healthy Vegan Mayo, WHAT? (page 147)

Put the chickpeas, chickpea liquid, oats, potato starch, sage, salt, pepper, fennel, garlic powder and allspice in a food processor. Pulse to mix, then add the apples. Pulse again slowly, and do not overmix. You want the mixture chunky but crumbly, not like hummus.

Place the mixture into a bowl, and put it in the fridge for at least 20 minutes; an hour is best. Making this the day before and letting it sit overnight is optimal. This helps all the flavors marinate and leads to a sturdier burger.

To cook, shape the mixture into patties. If you're not using a nonstick pan, then you may want to prepare the pan by brushing it with a tad of oil to avoid sticking. Place the patties in a pan on the stovetop over medium heat for 15 minutes on each side. Pans and stovetops vary, so begin to check the patties at 10 minutes. If you try to slide your spatula under a patty and it won't give, then it isn't ready and needs to cook longer.

You can also bake the patties on a parchment-lined cookie sheet at 375°F (191°C) for about 20 to 25 minutes on each side. Allow the patties to cool and set for 5 to 7 minutes.

Serve on rolls with the toppings of your choice.

Notes: The liquid from the can of chickpeas is also known as aquafaba. It is a binder that helps keep the patties together. I reserve it and freeze it in ice cube trays for future use.

For the fennel, I simply take regular dried fennel seed and crush it with the back of a spoon. This helps disperse the flavor better throughout the burgers.

Kids: Make patties into a smaller slider size or into nuggets. Serve mayo on the side as a dipper.

MARGARITA PIZZA BURGER

My two favorite foods come together to form one of my favorite burgers. With simple ingredients just like its pizza counterpart, this burger has an amazing texture. You don't need a lot for the perfect patty. Smother on extra pizza and cream sauce and get ready for flavor fireworks.

1 cup (200 g) cooked brown or green lentils

¼ cup (50 g) cooked or canned white beans (such as great northern beans), drained and rinsed

¼ cup (10 g) fresh basil

¼ cup (15 g) bread crumbs (gluten-free if needed)

½ cup (80 g) oats

¼ cup (62 g) Quick-and-Easy Pizza Sauce (page 152)

1 tsp dried thyme

1 tsp dried oregano

½ tsp garlic powder

1 tsp sea salt

1 cup (76 g) uncooked chopped mushrooms

TO SERVE

4 to 5 buns

Fresh basil

Tomato

Quick-and-Easy Pizza Sauce (page 152)

Cream Sauce for the Soul (page 159)

Place the lentils, beans, basil, bread crumbs, oats, pizza sauce, thyme, oregano, garlic powder and salt in a food processor and pulse until well chopped; you want a fine grainlike size. Add the mushrooms and pulse some more. Check to make sure the mixture sticks together, and if it doesn't, pulse some more.

Place the mixture into a bowl, and put it in the fridge for at least 20 minutes; an hour is best. Making this the day before and letting it sit overnight is optimal. This helps all the flavors marinate and leads to a sturdier burger.

To cook, shape the mixture into patties. If you're not using a nonstick pan, then you may want to prepare the pan by brushing it with a tad of oil to avoid sticking. Place the patties in a pan on the stovetop over medium heat for 15 minutes on each side. Pans and stovetops vary, so begin to check the patties at 10 minutes. If you try to slide your spatula under a patty and it won't give, then it isn't ready and needs to cook longer.

You can also bake the patties on a parchment-lined cookie sheet at 375°F (191°C) for about 20 to 25 minutes on each side. Allow the patties to cool and set for 5 to 7 minutes.

Serve on buns with the toppings of your choice.

Kids: Make patties into a smaller slider size or into nuggets. Serve sauces on the side as dippers.

MY BIG FAT GREEK BURGER

Move over gyro, there's a new sandwich in town. Much like a big Greek family, this burger is packed with flavor. Top this burger with traditional salad ingredients like cucumber, tomatoes and red onion, then smother with home-style tzatziki sauce and take one step closer to Greek perfection!

2¼ cups (453 g) cooked or canned chickpeas, drained and rinsed (reserve the liquid)

¾ cup (114 g) chopped red onion

6 tbsp (60 g) steel-cut oats (gluten-free if needed)

6 tbsp (23 g) bread crumbs (gluten-free if needed)

2½ tbsp (4 g) dried oregano

2 tbsp (30 ml) lemon juice

1½ tbsp (22 ml) liquid from the can of chickpeas (see notes)

1½ tbsp (14 g) fresh chopped garlic

1 tbsp (15 ml) tamari or soy sauce

1 tbsp (2 g) dried thyme

1 to 2 tsp (5 to 10 g) sea salt (see notes)

½ tsp ground black pepper

TO SERVE

4 to 5 buns

Yiayia's Authentic Tzatziki (page 160)

Sliced cucumber

Red onion

Tomato

Place the chickpeas, onion, oats, bread crumbs, oregano, lemon juice, chickpea liquid, garlic, tamari, thyme, salt and pepper in a food processor. Pulse until the mixture is finely chopped but not puréed. Use your hands to make sure the mixture sticks together when pressed. If it doesn't, pulse a few more times until it does.

Place the mixture into a bowl, and put it in the fridge for at least 20 minutes; an hour is best. Making this the day before and letting it sit overnight is optimal. This helps all the flavors marinate and leads to a sturdier burger.

To cook, shape the mixture into patties. If you're not using a nonstick pan, then you may want to prepare the pan by brushing it with a tad of oil to avoid sticking. Place the patties in a pan on the stovetop over medium heat for 15 minutes on each side. Pans and stovetops vary, so begin to check the patties at 10 minutes. If you try to slide your spatula under a patty and it won't give, then it isn't ready and needs to cook longer.

You can also bake the patties on a parchment-lined cookie sheet at 375°F (191°C) for about 20 to 25 minutes on each side. Allow the patties to cool and set for 5 to 7 minutes.

Serve on buns with the toppings of your choice.

Notes: The liquid from the can of chickpeas is also known as aquafaba. It is a binder that helps keep the patties together. I reserve it and freeze it in ice cube trays for future use.

You may need more or less salt depending on whether you use reduced-sodium or regular tamari or soy sauce.

Kids: Make patties into a smaller slider size or into nuggets. Serve with sauce as a dipper.

HAWAIIAN TERIYAKI BURGER

Say aloha to a happy dinner with this sweet and tangy burger. A great combination of various ingredients all rolled into a perfectly textured patty. Drizzle with sticky teriyaki sauce and make sure to grab a napkin, because we're about to get messy!

1½ cups (300 g) cooked or canned chickpeas, drained and rinsed (reserve the liquid)

6 tbsp (64 g) chopped red pepper

6 tbsp (19 g) sliced green onions

¼ cup (38 g) chopped carrots

¼ cup (40 g) steel-cut oats (gluten-free if needed)

1 tbsp (15 ml) liquid from the can of chickpeas (see note)

1 tbsp (10 g) potato starch (not potato flour)

1 tbsp (15 ml) Stovetop Tasty Teriyaki Sauce (page 163)

1 tsp sea salt

½ tsp garlic powder

TO SERVE

4 to 5 buns

Stovetop Tasty Teriyaki Sauce (page 163)

Pineapple rings

Microgreens or lettuce

Place the chickpeas, red pepper, green onions, carrots, oats, chickpea liquid, potato starch, teriyaki sauce, salt and garlic powder into a food processor. Pulse until the mixture is finely chopped but not puréed. Use your hands to make sure the mixture sticks together when pressed. If it doesn't, pulse a few more times until it does.

Place the mixture into a bowl, and put it in the fridge for at least 20 minutes; an hour is best. Making this the day before and letting it sit overnight is optimal. This helps all the flavors marinate and leads to a sturdier burger.

To cook, shape the mixture into patties. If you're not using a nonstick pan, then you may want to prepare the pan by brushing it with a tad of oil to avoid sticking. Place the patties in a pan on the stovetop over medium heat for 15 minutes on each side. Pans and stovetops vary, so begin to check the patties at 10 minutes. If you try to slide your spatula under a patty and it won't give, then it isn't ready and needs to cook longer.

You can also bake the patties on a parchment-lined cookie sheet at 375°F (191°C) for about 20 to 25 minutes on each side. Allow the patties to cool and set for 5 to 7 minutes.

Serve on buns with the toppings of your choice.

Note: The liquid from the can of chickpeas is also known as aquafaba. It is a binder that helps keep the patties together. I reserve it and freeze it in ice cube trays for future use.

Kids: Make patties into a smaller slider size or into nuggets. Serve sauce on the side as a dipper.

THE ALL-AMERICAN

A basic all-American burger without the meat or processed ingredients. Whether it's a summer BBQ or you're just feeling like eating some classic comfort food, this neutral-flavored patty goes with just about anything. Leave it to marinate overnight for the ultimate fast-food burger flavor.

¾ cup (151 g) cooked brown or green lentils

½ cup (80 g) oats (gluten-free if needed)

¾ cup (151 g) dried chickpeas, soaked overnight (see note)

¼ cup (38 g) chopped sweet or yellow onion

¼ cup (15 g) bread crumbs (gluten-free if needed)

3 tbsp (22 g) walnuts

2 tbsp (30 ml) yellow mustard

¾ tsp sea salt

½ tsp ground black pepper

⅛ tsp liquid smoke

¾ cup (57 g) uncooked chopped white or cremini mushrooms

TO SERVE

½ cup (76 g) chopped yellow or sweet onion

¼ to ½ cup (60 to 118 ml) low-sodium veggie broth or 1 tbsp (15 ml) your favorite oil, for sautéing

½ tsp salt

4 to 5 buns

Lettuce

Tomato

All-American Special Sauce (page 148)

Place the lentils, oats, chickpeas, onion, bread crumbs, walnuts, mustard, salt, pepper and liquid smoke in a food processor and pulse until well chopped. You want a fine grainlike size. Add the mushrooms and pulse some more. Check to make sure the mixture sticks together, and if it doesn't, pulse some more.

Place the mixture into a bowl, and put it in the fridge for at least 20 minutes; an hour is best. Making this the day before and letting it sit overnight is optimal. This helps all the flavors marinate and leads to a sturdier burger.

While you are waiting, you can make the sautéed onion topping, if using, by putting the onion, broth and salt in a pan and sautéing over medium-low heat until the onions are browned and all the liquid has evaporated, about 8 to 10 minutes. Add more broth if necessary.

To cook, shape the mixture into patties. If you're not using a nonstick pan, then you may want to prepare the pan by brushing it with a tad of oil to avoid sticking. Place the patties in a pan on the stovetop over medium heat for 15 minutes on each side. Pans and stovetops vary, so begin to check the patties at 10 minutes. If you try to slide your spatula under a patty and it won't give, then it isn't ready and needs to cook longer.

You can also bake the patties on a parchment-lined cookie sheet at 375°F (191°C) for about 20 to 25 minutes on each side. Allow the patties to cool and set for 5 to 7 minutes.

Serve on buns with the toppings of your choice.

Note: Make sure you soak your chickpeas overnight or for at least 6 hours.

Kids: Make patties into a smaller slider size or into nuggets. Serve sauce on the side as a dipper.

THAI PEANUT PERFECTION

East meets West in this peanut-themed Asian-inspired burger. Because who doesn't love peanut butter when it can be paired with loads of veggies, amazing spices and formed into an all-in-one healthy meal? If you love peanut flavor, then you will love this fun twist!

1½ cups (300 g) cooked or canned chickpeas, drained and rinsed

½ cup (80 g) oats (gluten-free if needed)

½ cup (25 g) sliced green onion

½ cup (85 g) chopped red pepper

¼ cup (38 g) chopped carrots

¼ cup (40 g) peanuts

¼ cup (10 g) fresh cilantro

2 tbsp (30 ml) Skinny Peanut Sauce (page 143)

1 tbsp (10 g) chopped garlic

3 tsp (15 ml) tamari or soy sauce (see note)

2 tsp (10 ml) fresh lime juice

1 to 1½ tsp (5 to 8 g) sea salt (see note)

½ tsp ground ginger

TO SERVE

4 to 5 buns

Skinny Peanut Sauce (page 143)

Sliced red peppers

Shredded carrots

Shredded red and green cabbage

Cilantro

Place the chickpeas, oats, green onion, red pepper, carrots, peanuts, cilantro, peanut sauce, garlic, tamari, lime juice, salt and ginger into a food processor. Pulse until the mixture is finely chopped but not puréed. Check to make sure the mixture sticks together, and if it doesn't, pulse some more.

Place the mixture into a bowl, and put it in the fridge for at least 20 minutes; an hour is best. Making this the day before and letting it sit overnight is optimal. This helps all the flavors marinate and leads to a sturdier burger.

To cook, shape the mixture into patties. If you're not using a nonstick pan, then you may want to prepare the pan by brushing it with a tad of oil to avoid sticking. Place the patties in a pan on the stovetop over medium heat for 15 minutes on each side. Pans and stovetops vary, so begin to check the patties at 10 minutes. If you try to slide your spatula under a patty and it won't give, then it isn't ready and needs to cook longer.

You can also bake the patties on a parchment-lined cookie sheet at 375°F (191°C) for about 20 to 25 minutes on each side. Allow the patties to cool and set for 5 to 7 minutes.

Serve on buns with the toppings of your choice.

Note: You may need more or less salt depending on whether you use reduced-sodium or regular tamari or soy sauce. To give these a sweet rather than salty flavor, substitute the tamari or soy sauce with coconut aminos.

Kids: Make patties into a smaller slider size or into nuggets. Serve sauce on the side as a dipper.

THREE-BEAN CHILI BURGER

Three types of protein in one flavor-packed burger. Ditch the bowl and grab some buns, top with your favorite traditional chili toppings and devour.

¾ cup (151 g) cooked brown or green lentils

½ cup (80 g) oats (gluten-free if needed)

¼ cup (50 g) cooked or canned black beans, drained and rinsed (see note)

¼ cup (50 g) cooked or canned kidney beans, drained and rinsed (see note)

¼ cup (15 g) bread crumbs (gluten-free if needed)

¼ cup (38 g) chopped carrots

¼ cup (43 g) chopped red pepper

¼ cup (38 g) chopped red onion

3 tbsp (50 g) tomato paste

2½ tsp (6 g) smoked paprika

2½ tsp (6 g) dried chili powder

2 tsp (5 g) dried cumin

1½ tsp (7.5 g) sea salt

TO SERVE

4 to 5 buns

THE Vegan Sour Cream (page 144)

Avocado

Corn chips

Lettuce

Place the lentils, oats, black beans, kidney beans, bread crumbs, carrots, red pepper, red onion, tomato paste, paprika, chili powder, cumin and salt in a food processor and pulse until everything is well chopped. You want a fine grain size. Check to make sure the mixture sticks together, and if it doesn't, pulse some more.

Place the mixture into a bowl, and put it in the fridge for at least 20 minutes; an hour is best. Making this the day before and letting it sit overnight is optimal. This helps all the the flavors marinate and leads to a sturdier burger.

To cook, shape the mixture into patties. If you're not using a nonstick pan, then you may want to prepare the pan by brushing it with a tad of oil to avoid sticking. Place the patties in a pan on the stovetop and cook over medium heat for 15 minutes on each side. Pans and stovetops vary, so begin to check the patties at 10 minutes. If you try to slide your spatula under a patty and it won't give, then it isn't ready and needs to cook longer.

You can also bake the patties on a parchment-lined cookie sheet at 375°F (191°C) for about 20 to 25 minutes on each side. Allow the patties to cool and set for 5 to 7 minutes.

Serve on buns with the toppings of your choice.

Note: The variety of beans is what makes this burger, but in a pinch, you can use only one kind; just make sure the total amount of beans used is the same.

Kids: Make patties into a smaller slider size or into nuggets. Serve sour cream on the side as a dipper.

CAULIFLOWER "FISH" BURGER

This simple and flavorful burger with a lemon tang is a whole food, plant-based way to feed that fish sandwich craving. It's topped with the creamiest dill sauce you've ever had. Warning! Extreme sauce addiction may occur. Another one-stop meal to get in all you need!

1½ cups (300 g) cooked or canned chickpeas, drained and rinsed (reserve the liquid)

1½ cups (344 g) chopped cauliflower

3 tbsp (18 g) almond flour (see notes)

3 tbsp (32 g) cornmeal

3 tbsp (11 g) bread crumbs (gluten-free if needed)

2 tbsp (30 ml) liquid from the can of chickpeas (see notes)

1½ tbsp (22 ml) lemon juice

1½ tsp (1 g) dried parsley

1½ tsp (3 g) garlic powder

1½ tsp (7 g) sea salt

TO SERVE

4 to 5 buns

Creamy Dill with a Tangy Twist (page 151)

Hot sauce

Shredded cabbage

Put all of the chickpeas, cauliflower, almond flour, cornmeal, bread crumbs, chickpea liquid, lemon juice, parsley, garlic powder and salt in a food processor and pulse to incorporate. Pulse slowly and do not overmix. You want the mixture crumbly, not like hummus. Check to make sure the mixture sticks together, and if it doesn't, pulse some more.

Place the mixture into a bowl, and put it in the fridge for at least 20 minutes; an hour is best. Making this the day before and letting it sit overnight is optimal. This helps all the flavors marinate and leads to a sturdier burger.

To cook, shape the mixture into patties. If you're not using a nonstick pan, then you may want to prepare the pan by brushing it with a tad of oil to avoid sticking. Place the patties in a pan on the stovetop over medium heat for 15 minutes on each side. Pans and stovetops vary, so begin to check the patties at 10 minutes. If you try to slide your spatula under a patty and it won't give, then it isn't ready and needs to cook longer.

You can also bake the patties on a parchment-lined cookie sheet at 375°F (191°C) for about 20 to 25 minutes on each side. Allow the patties to cool and set for 5 to 7 minutes.

Serve on buns with the toppings of your choice.

Notes: I use a fine-ground blanched almond flour, but because this isn't a baked good, any almond flour would work.

The liquid from the can of chickpeas is also known as aquafaba. It is a binder that helps keep the patties together. I reserve it and freeze it in ice cube trays for future use.

Kids: Make patties into a smaller slider size or into nuggets. Serve sauce on the side as a dipper.

DOWN-HOME BBQ

Bringing BBQ to your table the nontraditional way. No animals were harmed in this hearty meal, but all of your taste buds will party at the first bite. Slather on as much BBQ sauce as you want and grab a napkin—it's going to get messy. Hope you aren't wearing white!

1 cup (160 g) cooked brown rice

1 cup (200 g) cooked or canned black beans, drained and rinsed

½ cup (75 g) chopped sweet or yellow onion (see notes)

¼ cup (50 g) cooked chopped potato (see notes)

2 tbsp (22 g) cornmeal

1 tbsp (15 ml) Easy Homemade BBQ Sauce (page 156)

2 tsp (5 g) garlic powder

2 tsp (5 g) chili powder

1½ tsp (7 ml) liquid smoke

1 tsp sea salt

1 tsp maple syrup

¼ to ½ cup (36 to 72 g) cooked frozen corn (defrosted to room temp) or fresh corn (add less or more per your preference)

TO SERVE

4 to 5 buns

Lightly grilled rings of sweet or yellow onion

Lettuce

Tomato

Easy Homemade BBQ Sauce (page 156)

Place the rice, beans, onion, potato, cornmeal, BBQ sauce, garlic powder, chili powder, liquid smoke, salt and syrup into a food processor. Pulse a few times until chunky. Add the corn and pulse a few more times. Don't overpulse or the mixture will get too soft and diplike.

Place the mixture into a bowl, and put it in the fridge for at least 20 minutes; an hour is best. Making this the day before and letting it sit overnight is optimal. This helps all the flavors marinate and leads to a sturdier burger.

To cook, shape the mixture into patties. If you're not using a nonstick pan, then you may want to prepare the pan by brushing it with a tad of oil to avoid sticking. Place the patties in a pan on the stovetop over medium heat for 15 minutes on each side. Pans and stovetops vary, so begin to check the patties at 10 minutes. If you try to slide your spatula under a patty and it won't give, then it isn't ready and needs to cook longer.

You can also bake the patties on a parchment-lined cookie sheet at 375°F (191°C) for about 20 to 25 minutes on each side. Allow the patties to cool and set for 5 to 7 minutes.

Serve on buns with the toppings of your choice.

Notes: Save some rings of onion to use as an optional topping. Cook the onion after you sauté the burger ingredients.

Any type of starchy potato works—I use red. Sweet potato is not recommended as it is not starchy enough. Cook the potato in the microwave or oven. I don't recommend boiling it because it makes the potato too wet. Measure the potato by mashing it into the measuring cup.

Kids: Make patties into a smaller slider size or into nuggets. Serve sauce on the side as a dipper.

TOMATO LOVERS' PARADISE

Layers upon layers of tomato fill this super flavorful burger. From sauce to dried to fresh, this is tomato karma extreme! My husband declared this was his favorite burger yet.

1½ cups (300 g) cooked brown or green lentils

1 cup (40 g) uncooked chopped spinach

1 cup (165 g) chopped sun-dried tomatoes, soaked in water and softened if dry (see notes)

½ cup (100 g) cooked or canned white beans (such as great northern beans), drained and rinsed

½ cup (20 g) fresh basil

½ cup (80 g) oats (gluten-free if needed)

6 tbsp (88 ml) Quick-and-Easy Pizza Sauce (page 152)

2 tsp (1 g) dried oregano

1 tsp garlic powder

1 tsp sea salt (see notes)

TO SERVE

4 to 5 buns

Tomato

Spinach

Quick-and-Easy Pizza Sauce (page 152)

Place the lentils, spinach, tomatoes, beans, basil, oats, sauce, oregano, garlic powder and salt in a food processor and pulse until well chopped. You want a fine grainlike size. Check to make sure the mixture sticks together, and if it doesn't, pulse some more.

Place the mixture into a bowl, and put it in the fridge for at least 20 minutes; an hour is best. Making this the day before and letting it sit overnight is optimal. This helps all flavors marinate and leads to a sturdier burger.

To cook, shape the mixture into patties. If you're not using a nonstick pan, then you may want to prepare the pan by brushing it with a tad of oil to avoid sticking. Place the patties in a pan on the stovetop over medium heat for 15 minutes on each side. Pans and stovetops vary, so begin to check the patties at 10 minutes. If you try to slide your spatula under a patty and it won't give, then it isn't ready and needs to cook longer.

You can also bake the patties on a parchment-lined cookie sheet at 375°F (191°C) for about 20 to 25 minutes on each side. Allow the patties to cool and set for 5 to 7 minutes.

Serve on buns with the toppings of your choice.

Notes: Make sure you get sun-dried tomatoes that are dried or in water, not in oil.

Adjust the amount of salt depending on how salty your sun-dried tomatoes are.

Kids: Make patties into a smaller slider size or into nuggets. Serve sauce on the side as a dipper.

FOOTBALL IN A BUN

Think you can't put sports in a bun? Well, I did! Bringing you the best of game day nuzzled nicely between two pieces of bread, ready to be devoured. Potato chips, onion dip, veggies and protein all come together for this ultimate sporty meal. Sound weird? Probably, but weird can be tasty!

1½ cups (345 g) chopped cauliflower (see notes)

1¼ cups (250 g) cooked or canned white beans (such as great northern beans), drained and rinsed

¼ cup (38 g) chopped carrots (see notes)

¼ cup (50 g) minced onion flakes

2 tbsp (20 g) chopped celery (see notes)

1 tbsp (15 g) Ultimate Onion Dip (page 140)

1 tbsp (8 g) onion powder

2 tsp (1 g) dried parsley

1 tsp garlic powder

1 tsp sea salt

½ tsp celery seed

1 cup (22 g) crushed potato chips

TO SERVE

4 to 5 buns (see notes)

Red onion

Shredded carrots

Ultimate Onion Dip (page 140)

Potato chips

Lettuce

Place the cauliflower, beans, carrots, onion flakes, celery, dip, onion powder, parsley, garlic powder, salt and celery seed in a food processor and pulse until chopped. Add the potato chips and pulse again until you get a fine grainlike size. Check to make sure the mixture sticks together, and if it doesn't, pulse some more. Do not overpulse or it will become mush.

Place the mixture into a bowl, and put it in the fridge for at least 20 minutes; an hour is best. Making this the day before and letting it sit overnight is optimal. This helps all the flavors marinate and leads to a sturdier burger.

To cook, shape the mixture into patties. If you're not using a nonstick pan, then you may want to prepare the pan by brushing it with a tad of oil to avoid sticking. Place the patties in a pan on the stovetop over medium heat for 15 minutes on each side. Pans and stovetops vary, so begin to check the patties at 10 minutes. If you try to slide your spatula under a patty and it won't give, then it isn't ready and needs to cook longer.

You can also bake the patties on a parchment-lined cookie sheet at 375°F (191°C) for about 20 to 25 minutes on each side. Allow the patties to cool and set for 5 to 7 minutes.

Serve on buns with the toppings of your choice.

Notes: The cauliflower, carrots and celery are roughly chopped for measuring purposes. They will be chopped again in the food processor.

For the buns, it is recommended to use a softer bun. A hard or crisp one will squish the burger more, whereas a softer bun will help keep the texture of the burger since this is a more delicate burger.

Kids: Make patties into a smaller slider size or into nuggets. Serve sauce on the side as a dipper.

ULTIMATE "MEATBALL" BURGER

This hearty burger will fulfill any meat lover. Stuffed with greens and loads of protein, then topped with the perfect homemade pizza sauce, it's an all-in-one type of meal! From the first bite to the last, you'll love the warm, comforting flavor of this burger, kind of like being wrapped in your favorite cozy blanket.

2 cups (151 g) chopped mushrooms

2 cups (260 g) chopped kale, stems removed

1 tbsp (10 g) chopped garlic

Low-sodium veggie broth (about ½ cup [118 ml]) or drizzle of oil, for sautéing

1½ cups (300 g) cooked brown or green lentils

½ cup (30 g) bread crumbs (gluten-free if needed)

½ cup (80 g) oats (gluten-free if needed)

¼ cup (30 g) chopped walnuts

¼ cup (62 g) Quick-and-Easy Pizza Sauce (page 152)

1 tbsp (2 g) dried thyme

1 tbsp (2 g) dried basil

1 tbsp (2 g) dried oregano

1 tsp sea salt

TO SERVE

4 to 5 buns

Quick-and-Easy Pizza Sauce (page 152)

Chopped sautéed kale

Sauté the mushrooms, kale and garlic with broth or oil over medium heat until the mushrooms are soft and the liquid has evaporated, about 10 to 15 minutes. Set aside.

Place the the lentils, bread crumbs, oats, walnuts, sauce, thyme, basil, oregano and salt in a food processor and pulse until well chopped. You want a crumblelike texture. Check to make sure the mixture sticks together, and if it doesn't, pulse some more, but make sure it doesn't turn into a purée. You can also add a bit more pizza sauce if it doesn't stick yet, however, you don't want it to be too wet.

Place the mushrooms, kale and garlic into the processor, making sure not to add any leftover juices, and pulse a few times until everything is well chopped and incorporated. If the ingredients aren't mixed after a few pulses, put the mixture in a bowl and mix it with your hands.

Place the mixture into a bowl, and put it in the fridge for at least 20 minutes; an hour is best. Making this the day before and letting it sit overnight is optimal. This helps all flavors marinate and leads to a sturdier burger.

To cook, shape the mixture into patties. If you're not using a nonstick pan, then you may want to prepare the pan by brushing it with a tad of oil to avoid sticking. Place the patties in a pan on the stovetop over medium heat for 15 minutes on each side. Pans and stovetops vary, so begin to check the patties at 10 minutes. If you try to slide your spatula under a patty and it won't give, then it isn't ready and needs to cook longer.

You can also bake the patties on a parchment-lined cookie sheet at 375°F (191°C) for about 20 to 25 minutes on each side. Allow the patties to cool and set for 5 to 7 minutes.

Serve on buns with the toppings of your choice.

Kids: Make patties into a smaller slider size or into nuggets. Serve sauce on the side as a dipper.

FAJITA YOUR BURGER

Get your veggies, protein and Mexican flavor all-in-one easy-to-put-together meal. Load it up with traditional fajita toppings and enjoy a Mexican-inspired meal in an easy-to-eat recipe. Olé!

1¼ cups (200 g) cooked brown rice

¾ cup (130 g) chopped red, yellow, green pepper mix (see notes)

6 tbsp (57 g) chopped red onion (see notes)

4 tsp (10 g) chili powder

2 tsp (5 g) paprika

2 tsp (5 g) garlic powder

1 tsp cumin

2 to 2½ tsp (10 to 13 g) sea salt (see notes)

6 tbsp (76 g) cooked chopped potato (see notes)

1 cup (200 g) cooked or canned black beans, rinsed and drained

4½ tbsp (48 g) cornmeal

3 tbsp (30 g) World's Best Roasted Salsa (page 132)

TO SERVE

4 to 5 buns

Mashed avocado

Extra sautéed peppers and onions

Shredded lettuce

Place the rice, peppers, onion, chili powder, paprika, garlic powder, cumin and salt into a food processor. Pulse until chopped well but not puréed. Add the potato, and pulse a few more times. Add the beans, cornmeal and salsa, and pulse only a few times to incorporate (about 4 to 5 times). Don't overpulse or the mixture will get too soft, gooey and diplike. Instead, put it in a bowl and mix it with your hands.

Place the mixture into a bowl, and put it in the fridge for at least 20 minutes; an hour is best. Making this the day before and letting it sit overnight is optimal. This helps all flavors marinate and leads to a sturdier burger.

To cook, shape the mixture into patties. If you're not using a nonstick pan, then you may want to prepare the pan by brushing it with a tad of oil to avoid sticking. Place the patties in a pan on the stovetop over medium heat for 15 minutes on each side. Pans and stovetops vary, so begin to check the patties at 10 minutes. If you try to slide your spatula under a patty and it won't give, then it isn't ready and needs to cook longer.

You can also bake the patties on a parchment-lined cookie sheet at 375°F (191°C) for about 20 to 25 minutes on each side. Allow the patties to cool and set for 5 to 7 minutes.

Serve on buns with the toppings of your choice.

Notes: Chop some extra peppers and red onion to use as an optional topping. While the burgers are setting, sauté the extra peppers and onion with veggie broth or a drizzle of oil and a pinch of salt until cooked throughout, about 8 to 10 minutes.

Any type of starchy potato works—I use red. Sweet potato is not recommended as it is not starchy enough. Cook the potato in the microwave or oven. I don't recommend boiling it because it makes the potato too wet. Measure the potato by mashing it into the measuring spoon.

Kids: Make patties into a smaller slider size or into nuggets. Serve sauce on the side as a dipper.

TEX-MEX FOR THE WIN

Tex-Mex flavor coming in hot! These burgers are stuffed with goodness and insane flavor with the combination of jalapeño slices, fresh cilantro, enchilada sauce and spices. It's kind of like nachos meets chili meets burritos. How can that be wrong?

1½ cups (242 g) cooked brown rice

6 tbsp (64 g) chopped red pepper

6 tbsp (64 g) chopped mild jalapeño slices (see notes)

6 tbsp (57 g) red onion

3 tbsp (8 g) chopped cilantro

3 tsp (8 g) chili powder

1½ tsp (4 g) cumin

1½ tsp (8 g) sea salt

6 tbsp (76 g) cooked chopped potato (see notes)

1 cup (200 g) cooked or canned pinto beans, drained and rinsed

4½ tbsp (48 g) cornmeal

2 tbsp (30 ml) No-Cook Enchilada Sauce (page 155)

TO SERVE

4 to 5 buns

No-Cook Enchilada Sauce (page 155)

Mild jalapeño slices

Avocado

Lettuce

Place the rice, red pepper, jalapeño slices, onion, cilantro, chili powder, cumin and salt into a food processor. Pulse until chopped well but not puréed. Add the potato and pulse a few more times. Add the beans, cornmeal and enchilada sauce, and pulse only a few times to incorporate (about 4 to 5 times). Don't overpulse or the mixture will get too soft, gooey and diplike. You can also put it in a bowl and mix it with your hands. Place the mixture into a bowl, and put it in the fridge for at least 20 minutes; an hour is best. Making this the day before and letting it sit overnight is optimal. This helps all the flavors marinate and leads to a sturdier burger.

To cook, shape the mixture into patties. If you're not using a nonstick pan, then you may want to prepare the pan by brushing it with a tad of oil to avoid sticking. Place the patties in a pan on the stovetop over medium heat for 15 minutes on each side. Pans and stovetops vary, so begin to check the patties at 10 minutes. If you try to slide your spatula under a patty and it won't give, then it isn't ready and needs to cook longer.

You can also bake the patties on a parchment-lined cookie sheet at 375°F (191°C) for about 20 to 25 minutes on each side. Allow the patties to cool and set for 5 to 7 minutes. Serve on buns with the toppings of your choice.

Notes: Make sure to drain the jalapeño slices before chopping as they are in liquid and very wet. If you don't drain them well, it will add too much liquid to the burger and the texture will be a bit mushier.

Any type of starchy potato works—I use red. Sweet potato is not recommended as it is not starchy enough. Cook the potato in the microwave or oven. I don't recommend boiling it because it makes the potato too wet. Measure the potato by mashing it into the measuring spoon.

Kids: Use mild jalapeño slices or reduce the amount. Make patties into a smaller slider size or into nuggets. Serve sauce on the side as a dipper.

A CURRY BURGER FOR ALL

A curry burger for non-curry lovers. Truth be told, curry is not a favorite flavor of mine, so I created a burger that even I would eat. Adjust the curry seasoning to the level of curry lover you are, top with creamy curry sauce and dig in! You will love the exotic and aromatic flavor these burgers bring.

1½ cups (300 g) cooked or canned chickpeas, drained and rinsed

½ cup (80 g) oats (gluten-free if needed)

¼ cup (15 g) bread crumbs (gluten-free if needed)

¼ cup (38 g) chopped carrots

¼ cup (43 g) chopped red pepper

¼ cup (13 g) sliced green onion

2 to 4 tbsp (30 to 60 ml) Low-Fat Creamy Curry Sauce (page 136)

2 tbsp (5 g) fresh cilantro

2 to 4 tsp (7 to 15 g) curry powder (depending on personal preference)

1½ tsp (8 g) sea salt

½ tsp garlic powder

½ cup (100 g) cooked sweet potato (see note)

TO SERVE

4 to 5 buns

Low-Fat Creamy Curry Sauce (page 136)

Sliced red or green cabbage and carrots

Chopped red pepper

Cilantro

Place the chickpeas, oats, bread crumbs, carrots, red pepper, green onion, curry sauce, cilantro, curry powder, salt and garlic powder in a food processor and pulse until well chopped; you want a fine grainlike size. Add the sweet potato and pulse some more. Check to make sure the mixture sticks together, and if it doesn't, pulse some more.

Place the mixture into a bowl, and put it in the fridge for at least 20 minutes; an hour is best. Making this the day before and letting it sit overnight is optimal. This helps all the flavors marinate and leads to a sturdier burger.

To cook, shape the mixture into patties. If you're not using a nonstick pan, then you may want to prepare the pan by brushing it with a tad of oil to avoid sticking. Place the patties in a pan on the stovetop over medium heat for 15 minutes on each side. Pans and stovetops vary, so begin to check the patties at 10 minutes. If you try to slide your spatula under a patty and it won't give, then it isn't ready and needs to cook longer.

You can also bake the patties on a parchment-lined cookie sheet at 375°F (191°C) for about 20 to 25 minutes on each side. Allow the patties to cool and set for 5 to 7 minutes.

Serve on buns with the toppings of your choice.

Note: Cook the sweet potato in the microwave or oven. I don't recommend boiling it because it makes the potato too wet. Orange sweet potato is more moist than the white one, so you may need to adjust the amount of sauce depending on which type of sweet potato you use. Start with 2 tablespoons (30 ml) and add more as needed to help the patties stick together. Keep in mind that the longer you let the mixture sit, the drier it can get, so if you are not making the patties until the next day, you may want to add a touch more sauce.

Kids: Use only a touch of curry powder. Make patties into a smaller slider size or into nuggets. Serve sauce on the side as a dipper, but make sure the sauce is made mild.

GET YOUR GREENS

Get your dose of greens in this veggie-packed burger! Green juice, what? Filling, healthy and super yum. Make it into bite-size pieces and dip in ranch for the little ones' daily veggie fill. Heck, pop a few of those mini bites in your mouth too!

½ cup (80 g) oats (gluten-free if needed)

½ cup (93 g) sunflower seeds

½ cup (30 g) bread crumbs

2 cups (460 g) roughly chopped broccoli

2 cups (80 g) packed spinach

½ cup (76 g) chopped sweet or yellow onion

½ cup (20 g) packed basil

2 tbsp (30 ml) Vegan Ranch—The Real Deal (page 131)

1 tsp sea salt

½ tsp garlic powder

¼ tsp ground black pepper

TO SERVE

4 to 5 buns

Vegan Ranch—The Real Deal (page 131)

Red onion

Avocado

Sprouts

Pulse the oats and sunflower seeds in a food processor and add to a large bowl. Add the bread crumbs to the bowl.

Pulse the broccoli into small pieces and add them to the bowl.

Next, pulse the spinach, onion and basil. Add them to the bowl.

Put the vegan ranch, salt, garlic powder and pepper in the bowl and mix well.

Place the bowl in the fridge for at least 20 minutes; an hour is best. Making this the day before and letting it sit overnight is optimal. This helps all the flavors marinate and leads to a sturdier burger.

The mixture may look crumbly, but once you pack it into a patty it sticks together well. If it is falling apart, then your veggies were on the drier side so you may need to add a touch of water to the mixture, or you can add a little bit more of the ranch sauce. Add 1 teaspoon at a time until the mixture holds together.

To cook, shape the mixture into patties. If you're not using a nonstick pan, then you may want to prepare the pan by brushing it with a tad of oil to avoid sticking. Place the patties in a pan on the stovetop over medium heat for 15 minutes on each side. Pans and stovetops vary, so begin to check the patties at 10 minutes. If you try to slide your spatula under a patty and it won't give, then it isn't ready and needs to cook longer.

You can also bake the patties on a parchment-lined cookie sheet at 375°F (191°C) for about 20 to 25 minutes on each side. Allow the patties to cool and set for 5 to 7 minutes.

Serve on buns with the toppings of your choice.

Kids: Make patties into a smaller slider size or into nuggets. Serve sauce on the side as a dipper.

SWEET POTATO ENCHILADA BURGER

What happens when an enchilada ditches its tortilla and climbs into a bun? These amazing burgers, filled with wholesome ingredients and a combination of sweet, spicy and smoky flavors. Slather on the sauce and go to town, because no knife or fork is needed to devour these bad boys.

1 cup (161 g) cooked brown rice

¾ cup (135 g) chopped spinach

½ cup (25 g) sliced green onion

3 tbsp (8 g) chopped cilantro

3 tsp (8 g) chili powder

3 tsp (8 g) smoked paprika

2 tsp (5 g) cumin

1½ tsp (8 g) sea salt

½ cup (100 g) cooked chopped sweet potato (see note)

1 cup (200 g) cooked or canned black beans, drained and rinsed

3 tbsp (32 g) cornmeal

2 to 3 tbsp (30 to 45 ml) No-Cook Enchilada Sauce (page 155)

TO SERVE

4 to 5 buns

THE Vegan Sour Cream (page 144)

No-Cook Enchilada Sauce (page 155)

Avocado

Cilantro

Shredded lettuce

Place the rice, spinach, onion, cilantro, chili powder, paprika, cumin and salt into a food processor. Pulse until chopped well but not puréed. Add the potato and pulse a few more times. Add the beans, cornmeal and enchilada sauce, and pulse only a few times to incorporate (about 4 to 5 times). Don't overpulse or the mixture will get too soft, gooey and diplike. Instead, put it in a bowl and mix it with your hands.

Place the mixture into a bowl, and put it in the fridge for at least 20 minutes; an hour is best. Making this the day before and letting it sit overnight is optimal. This helps all flavors marinate and leads to a sturdier burger.

To cook, shape the mixture into patties. If you're not using a nonstick pan, then you may want to prepare the pan by brushing it with a tad of oil to avoid sticking. Place the patties in a pan on the stovetop over medium heat for 15 minutes on each side. Pans and stovetops vary, so begin to check the patties at 10 minutes. If you try to slide your spatula under a patty and it won't give, then it isn't ready and needs to cook longer.

You can also bake the patties on a parchment-lined cookie sheet at 375°F (191°C) for about 20 to 25 minutes on each side. Allow the patties to cool and set for 5 to 7 minutes.

Serve on buns with the toppings of your choice.

Note: Cook the potato in the microwave or oven. I don't recommend boiling it because it makes the potato too wet. Measure the potato by mashing it into the measuring cup. Orange sweet potato is more moist than the white variety, so you may need to adjust the amount of sauce depending on which type of sweet potato you use. Start with 1 tablespoon (15 ml) and add more as needed to help the patties stick together and not seem too dry. Keep in mind that the longer you let the mixture sit, the drier it can get, so if you are not making the patties until the next day you may want to add a touch more sauce.

Kids: Make patties into a smaller slider size or into nuggets. Serve sauces on the side as dippers.

THE LOW-CARB PORTOBELLO

A low-carb burger for the carb lover in you. I created this burger to satisfy even the biggest carb fanatic. These have such a great combination of herby and tangy flavor and a range of different textures, you won't even miss the bread. Get messy and dig in with your hands, or choose the clean side and attack with a knife and fork. Either way this burger is so darn good!

PORTOBELLO MARINADE

2 cups (473 ml) veggie broth

½ cup (118 ml) balsamic vinegar

3 tbsp (45 ml) Dijon or brown mustard

1 tbsp (15 g) sea salt

1 tbsp (2 g) dried thyme

1 tbsp (2 g) dried rosemary

1 tbsp (8 g) garlic powder

8 small whole portobello mushrooms, stems removed

ZUCCHINI BATTER

1 zucchini

1 cup (97 g) almond flour (see note)

1 cup (240 ml) unsweetened, plain cashew or almond milk

ZUCCHINI BREADING

½ cup (85 g) cornmeal

¼ cup (24 g) almond flour (see note)

¼ cup (15 g) bread crumbs (gluten-free if needed)

2 tsp (10 g) sea salt

2 tsp (1 g) dried thyme

2 tsp (1 g) dried rosemary

2 tsp (5 g) garlic powder

ROSEMARY THYME MAYO

¼ cup (60 ml) Healthy Vegan Mayo, WHAT? (page 147)

1 tsp dried thyme

1 tsp dried rosemary

1 tsp balsamic vinegar

TO SERVE

Red onion

Microgreens

Avocado

Preheat the oven to 450°F (232°C).

In a bowl, mix the broth, vinegar, mustard, salt, thyme, rosemary and garlic powder, and whisk well until combined.

Place the portobello mushrooms in a shallow baking dish, and pour the marinade over the top. Allow the mushrooms to marinate while you prepare the zucchini.

Cut the zucchini in half width-wise. Cut a thin slice off of each long edge so that some of the skin is gone. Then slice each half lengthwise into 4 equal strips. You should have 8 flat rectangles.

Make the zucchini batter by whisking the almond flour and milk in a bowl until a thick batter forms.

Make the zucchini breading by mixing together the cornmeal, flour, bread crumbs, salt, thyme, rosemary and garlic powder in a shallow baking dish.

(continued)

THE LOW-CARB PORTOBELLO (CONT.)

Using one hand for the batter and one for breading (this helps avoid clumping of the breading), dip each zucchini piece in the batter, then place it in the breading dish and cover it with the breading. Then place each piece on a parchment-lined cookie sheet.

When you're done, place the mushrooms on a parchment-lined cookie sheet (use the same one if there is room). Bake the zucchini and mushrooms for 15 to 20 minutes. Check at 15 minutes and remove the mushrooms if they are done. Continue to bake the zucchini pieces until they're crispy, about 5 to 7 minutes.

While the vegetables are baking, make the rosemary thyme mayo. Mix the mayo with the thyme, rosemary and vinegar. Set it aside for serving.

Serve using two portobello mushrooms as buns. Slather one of the mushrooms with 1 tablespoon (15 ml) of rosemary thyme mayo. Fill the buns with the crispy zucchini, sliced red onion, microgreens and avocado.

Note: I use a fine-ground blanched almond flour, but because this isn't a baked good, any almond flour would work.

Kids: Cut into small pieces. Serve mayo on the side as a dipper.

I HEART MUSHROOMS

Using a variety of mushrooms is the key to the best flavor in this burger. I was going for the perfect ratio of mushroom to rice, with a pop of flavor, so they are a bit on the delicate side. It takes the right amount of chopping with the mushrooms, not too big so they fall apart, but not too small so they become a puréed mess. Flavors will be amazing either way!

½ cup (76 g) chopped sweet or yellow onion (see notes)

Low-sodium veggie broth (about ¾ cup [177 ml]), or drizzle of oil, divided, for sautéing

¾ tsp sea salt, divided

1 tbsp (10 g) chopped garlic

1 cup (161 g) cooked brown rice (see notes)

¾ cup (45 g) bread crumbs (gluten-free if needed)

¾ tsp dried thyme

¾ tsp dried oregano

3 cups (227 g) chopped portobello mushrooms (stems and gills removed, see notes)

3 cups (227 g) chopped cremini mushrooms (see notes)

TO SERVE

4 to 5 buns (see notes)

Healthy Vegan Mayo, WHAT? (page 147)

Sautéed mushrooms

Arugula

Lightly grilled rings of sweet or yellow onion

Sauté the onion in ¼ cup (60 ml) of broth and ¼ teaspoon of salt until the onions begin to get translucent and fragrant, about 4 to 5 minutes. Add garlic and sauté for about 1 to 2 minutes until the garlic is browned. Add to a food processor with the rice, bread crumbs, thyme, oregano and ¼ teaspoon salt. Pulse until the mixture is chopped and sticky. You want to make sure to pulse enough so that the starch in the rice is activated in order for the burgers to stick together well.

Next, prepare the mushrooms. Make sure when chopping the mushrooms that you chop them big enough so you see chunks of mushroom in the final burger, but small enough to allow the mixture to stick together. Aim for between pea-size to cooked chickpea-size. Sauté the chopped mushrooms over medium-high heat with the remaining ½ cup (118 ml) of broth and the remaining ¼ teaspoon of salt until cooked well and no juices remain, about 10 to 15 minutes. Add to the food processor (making sure not to add any small amount of leftover liquid) and pulse 3 to 4 times. Do not overpulse or the mushrooms will purée, and you will have a wet, mushy burger. You want to see mushroom chunks in the final result.

Place the mixture into a bowl, and put it in the fridge for at least 20 minutes; an hour is best. Making this the day before and letting it sit overnight is optimal. This helps all flavors marinate and leads to a sturdier burger.

Shape the mixture into patties, making sure to firmly pack them in. The starch in the rice will help them stick well.

Because of how delicate these burgers can be, I suggest baking over cooking on the stovetop. Bake on a parchment-lined cookie sheet at 375°F (191°C) for about 20 to 25 minutes on each side. Be careful when flipping. If they seem too soft to flip, then cook them for a bit longer, just adjust the cooking time on the second side as well, so each side is cooked for the same amount of time. Allow to cool and set for 5 to 7 minutes.

(continued)

I HEART MUSHROOMS (CONT.)

You can also cook these patties in a pan—you just need to be careful when handling them and use a spatula to help them keep their shape as they cook. If you don't use a nonstick pan, then you may want to prepare the pan by brushing it with a tad of oil to avoid sticking. Cook in a pan on the stovetop over medium heat for 15 minutes on each side. Pans and stovetops vary, so begin to check the patties at 10 minutes. If you try to slide your spatula under a patty and it won't give, then it isn't ready and needs to cook longer. These are a more delicate burger so be careful when flipping.

Serve on buns with the toppings of your choice.

Notes: Save some rings of onion and chop some extra mushrooms to use as an optional topping. Cook these after you sauté the burger ingredients.

Make sure that your rice isn't wet after cooking. This will cause the burger not to stick together very well. You want the rice cooked well so that the starch will activate when pulsed in the food processor. This is what gets the burgers to stick together.

Clean the portobello mushrooms by using a spoon to scrape out the underneath brown gills. You can use white mushrooms in place of the cremini, however cremini have a little more flavor.

I recommend using a soft bun. A hard or really crisp bun will squish the burger more, whereas a softer bun will help keep the texture of the burger since this is a more delicate burger.

Kids: Make patties into a smaller slider size or into nuggets. Use mayo on the side as a dipper.

Yield: 4 TO 5
BURGERS

Level: 3

CRABLESS CAKE BURGER

Feeling the need for something light? Ditch the bun and serve this on a bed of shredded cabbage and then drizzle with sauce.

½ cup (25 g) chopped green onion (about 2 green onions)

½ cup (76 g) chopped celery

1 (14-oz [397-g]) can artichoke hearts (see notes)

¾ cup (151 g) cooked or canned white beans (such as great northern beans), drained and rinsed

1 tbsp (2.5 g) fresh chopped parsley

¾ tsp sea salt

¼ tsp ground black pepper

¾ cup (45 g) bread crumbs (gluten-free if needed)

2 tbsp (28 g) Tartar Sauce Extreme (page 139)

1 tsp hot sauce, optional but highly recommended

TO SERVE

4 to 5 buns (see notes)

Tartar Sauce Extreme (page 139)

Hot sauce

Shredded cabbage

Add the green onion, celery and artichoke hearts to a food processor. Pulse until everything is chopped. Do not overmix; you want some larger pieces. Put the mixture in a bowl.

Next, add the beans, parsley, salt and pepper to the processor and pulse only a few times, around 3 to 4. Don't overpulse or you will get hummus. Put this mixture in the bowl with the artichoke heart mix.

Using a spatula, fold in the bread crumbs, tartar sauce and hot sauce, if using. Carefully mix to incorporate all ingredients, but don't overmix.

Put the bowl in the fridge for at least 20 minutes; an hour is best. Making this the day before and letting it sit overnight is optimal. This helps all flavors marinate and leads to a sturdier burger.

To cook, shape the mixture into patties. If you're not using a nonstick pan, then you may want to prepare the pan by brushing it with a tad of oil to avoid sticking. Place the patties in a pan on the stovetop over medium heat for 15 minutes on each side. Pans and stovetops vary, so begin to check the patties at 10 minutes. If you try to slide your spatula under a patty and it won't give, then it isn't ready and needs to cook longer.

You can also bake the patties on a parchment-lined cookie sheet at 375°F (191°C) for about 20 to 25 minutes on each side. Allow the patties to cool and set for 5 to 7 minutes. Serve on buns with the toppings of your choice.

Notes: You want the artichoke hearts to have as little liquid as possible. To get them nice and dry, squeeze the liquid out with your hands, then wrap the hearts in a paper towel and squeeze out more liquid until pretty dry.

For the buns, it is recommended to use a softer bun since this is a more delicate burger. A hard or crisp bun will squish the burger more, whereas a softer bun will help keep the texture of the burger.

Kids: Make patties into a smaller slider size or into nuggets. Serve sauce on the side as a dipper.

BUFFALO WING SLIDERS

Whether you're watching the game or satisfying a craving, you will love this vegan way to enjoy spicy buffalo sauce. I may or may not have eaten most of these in one sitting. Place the crispy cauliflower on the other side of the kitchen as you prep the rest of this recipe. This will avoid the disappointment of realizing you ate them all before you could serve dinner.

1 medium-size head cauliflower

¾ to 1 cup (177 to 240 ml) buffalo cayenne pepper hot sauce (I like Frank's Red Hot Buffalo Wings Sauce)

CRISPY COATING

¾ cup (128 g) cornmeal

¾ cup (45 g) bread crumbs (gluten-free if needed)

6 tbsp (60 g) hemp seeds or almond flour (see notes)

6 tsp (3 g) dried parsley

6 tsp (15 g) garlic powder

BATTER

2 cups (193 g) almond flour/meal

1 cup (240 ml) buffalo cayenne pepper hot sauce (I like Frank's Red Hot Buffalo Wings Sauce)

1 cup (240 ml) sparkling soda water

2 tsp (7 g) baking powder

Drizzle of oil, optional (see notes)

TO SERVE

4 to 5 slider-size buns

Vegan Ranch—The Real Deal (page 131)

Buffalo cayenne pepper hot sauce

Red onion

Lettuce

Preheat the oven to 450°F (232°C).

Slice the cauliflower into large slider-size pieces.

Make the crispy coating by mixing together the cornmeal, bread crumbs, hemp seeds, parsley and garlic powder, then place it in a shallow baking dish.

Make the batter by combining the almond flour, buffalo cayenne pepper hot sauce, water and baking powder in a bowl until fully mixed. Add a drizzle of oil if you'd like.

Using one hand for the batter and one for the coating (this helps avoid clumping of the coating), dip each cauliflower piece in the batter then place it in the coating dish and cover with coating. Place each piece on a parchment-lined cookie sheet. Make sure to evenly spread out the pieces.

Bake for about 25 minutes. Remove the cookie sheet from the oven and drizzle about ½ cup (120 ml) of hot sauce on top of the cauliflower pieces, trying to coat the top sides well. Using a pastry brush can help. Flip them over and drizzle the rest of the hot sauce on top of the other sides, trying to coat them well. Put them back in the oven and bake for 10 minutes until they're crispy.

Serve immediately on slider buns with the toppings of your choice, using 1 to 2 pieces of cauliflower for each slider, depending on size.

Notes: You can use almond flour instead of hemp seeds to make it easier, but I like the final texture the hemp seeds give because of their natural oils. I use a fine-ground blanched almond flour, but because this isn't a baked good, any almond flour would work.

You can add a small drizzle of oil to the batter if you want. It is definitely not needed but can add an extra crispness to the final product.

Kids: May be too spicy for kids.

AUTUMN BURGER

From sweet butternut squash to thyme and sea salt, the fall flavor intensity here has a "go big or go home" attitude. A little extra effort is truly worth it because these little patties are insanely delicious!

4 cups (719 g) chopped raw butternut squash

Low-sodium veggie broth (about 8 tbsp [118 ml]) or drizzle of oil, divided, for roasting

2 tsp (10 g) sea salt, divided

¾ cup (135 g) peeled and chopped apples

¾ cup (114 g) sliced leeks

1½ tbsp (14 g) chopped garlic

1½ tbsp (2.5 g) dried thyme

1½ cups (241 g) cooked brown rice

6 tbsp (55 g) pumpkin seeds

LEMON THYME MAYO

¼ cup (55 g) Healthy Vegan Mayo, WHAT? (page 147)

2 tsp (10 ml) lemon juice

1 tsp dried thyme

TO SERVE

4 to 5 buns

Arugula

Preheat the oven to 400°F (204°C).

In a large mixing bowl, mix the squash with 5 tablespoons (74 ml) of broth or a drizzle of oil and 1 teaspoon of salt. Place the squash on a parchment-lined cookie sheet and roast for 15 minutes.

Meanwhile, place the apples, leeks, garlic and thyme in the bowl and mix well with the other 3 tablespoons (45 ml) of broth or a drizzle of oil. Add this mixture to the cookie sheet with the roasted squash, mix around to incorporate and roast for 30 minutes.

While the vegetable mixture is roasting, place the rice, pumpkin seeds and the remaining 1 teaspoon of salt into a food processor. Pulse until chopped well.

To make the Lemon Thyme Mayo, combine Healthy Vegan Mayo, WHAT?, lemon juice and thyme in a small bowl and mix well. Set aside for serving.

Once the veggie mix is done roasting, allow it to cool a few minutes, then add the mix to the processor and pulse only a few times to incorporate. Don't overpulse.

Place the mixture into a bowl, and put it in the fridge for at least 20 minutes; an hour is best. Making this the day before and letting it sit overnight is optimal. This helps all flavors marinate and leads to a sturdier burger.

To cook, shape the mixture into patties. If you're not using a nonstick pan, then you may want to prepare the pan by brushing it with a tad of oil to avoid sticking. Place the patties in a pan on the stovetop over medium heat for 15 minutes on each side. Pans and stovetops vary, so begin to check the patties at 10 minutes. If you try to slide your spatula under a patty and it won't give, then it isn't ready and needs to cook longer.

You can also bake the patties on a parchment-lined cookie sheet at 375°F (191°C) for about 20 to 25 minutes on each side. Allow the patties to cool and set for 5 to 7 minutes. Serve on buns with the Lemon Thyme Mayo and toppings of your choice.

Kids: Make patties into a smaller slider size or into nuggets. Serve mayo on the side as a dipper.

FOR SPICE LOVERS ONLY

Calling all spice lovers! Get your taste buds ready because this spicy burger may bring on a fabulous addiction. Filled with peppers of all shapes and sizes, this is not for the weak. Can you handle the heat?

½ cup (85 g) chopped mixed hot peppers

¼ cup (38 g) chopped sweet or yellow onion

Low-sodium veggie broth (about ½ cup [118 ml]) or drizzle of oil, for sautéing

1 tbsp (10 g) chopped garlic

1 cup (161 g) cooked brown rice

5 tbsp (63 g) cooked chopped sweet potato (see notes)

¾ cup (151 g) cooked or canned black beans, drained and rinsed

2 to 4 tbsp (30 to 60 ml) your favorite hot sauce

3 tbsp (32 g) cornmeal

2 tbsp (5 g) fresh chopped cilantro

2 tsp (7 g) smoked paprika

½ tsp sea salt (see notes)

½ to 1 tsp chipotle powder, optional

TO SERVE

4 to 5 buns

Lettuce

Extra hot peppers (raw or sautéed)

Avocado

Hot sauce

World's Best Roasted Salsa (page 132)

Sauté the hot peppers and onion with broth or oil over medium heat until they begin to get soft, about 8 to 10 minutes. Add the garlic and sauté for about 1 to 2 minutes until the garlic is browned. Set aside.

Place the rice in a food processor and pulse until it's chopped. Add the sweet potato and pulse a few times until the potato is mixed well. Add the black beans, hot sauce, cornmeal, cilantro, paprika, salt, chipotle powder if desired and sautéed peppers and onion, and pulse a few times until chunky. Don't overpulse or the mixture will get too soft, gooey and diplike. Instead, put it in a bowl and mix it with your hands.

Place the mixture into a bowl, and put it in the fridge for at least 20 minutes; an hour is best. Making this the day before and letting it sit overnight is optimal. This helps all the flavors marinate and leads to a sturdier burger.

To cook, shape the mixture into patties. If you're not using a nonstick pan, then you may want to prepare the pan by brushing it with a tad of oil to avoid sticking. Place the patties in a pan on the stovetop over medium heat for 15 minutes on each side. Pans and stovetops vary, so begin to check the patties at 10 minutes. If you try to slide your spatula under a patty and it won't give, then it isn't ready and needs to cook longer.

You can also bake the patties on a parchment-lined cookie sheet at 375°F (191°C) for about 20 to 25 minutes on each side. Allow the patties to cool and set for 5 to 7 minutes. Serve on buns with the toppings of your choice.

Notes: Cook the sweet potato in the microwave or oven. I don't recommend boiling it because it makes the potato too wet. Keep in mind that the longer you let the mixture sit, the drier it can get, so if you are not making the patties until the next day, you may want to add a touch more sauce. You may need to adjust the amount of salt depending on the hot sauce you use, as some are saltier than others.

Kids: May be too spicy for kids.

NOT YOUR MAMA'S MEATLOAF

This is definitely not your mama's meatloaf. It's better! Enjoy all the flavor and deliciousness of traditional meatloaf in a plant-based patty made with all whole foods.

¼ cup (38 g) chopped sweet or yellow onion

Low-sodium veggie broth (about ½ cup [118 ml]) or drizzle of oil, for sautéing

¾ tsp sea salt

1 tbsp (10 g) chopped fresh garlic

¼ cup (38 g) chopped carrots

¼ cup (38 g) chopped celery

¼ cup (36 g) cooked corn (frozen or fresh)

¾ cup (151 g) cooked brown or green lentils

½ cup (80 g) oats (gluten-free if needed)

6 tbsp (75 g) dried chickpeas, soaked overnight (see notes)

¼ cup (60 ml) Easy Homemade BBQ Sauce (page 156)

¼ cup (50 g) cooked chopped potato (see notes)

3 tbsp (22 g) walnuts

3 tbsp (5 g) dried thyme

4 tsp (10 g) chili powder

TO SERVE

4 to 5 buns

Red onion slices

Extra corn

Easy Homemade BBQ Sauce (page 156)

Mashed cooked potatoes

Sauté the onions in a pan over medium heat with veggie broth (or oil) and salt until they begin to get soft, about 4 to 5 minutes. Add garlic and sauté for about 1 to 2 minutes until the garlic is browned. Add the carrots, celery and corn and sauté 2 to 3 more minutes until the carrots slightly soften. You don't want them overcooked.

Place the mixture into a food processor with the lentils, oats, chickpeas, BBQ Sauce, potatoes, walnuts, thyme and chili powder. Pulse until well chopped; you want a fine grainlike size. Check to make sure the mixture sticks together, and if it doesn't, pulse some more.

Place the mixture into a bowl, and put it in the fridge for at least 20 minutes; an hour is best. Making this the day before and letting it sit overnight is optimal. This helps all the flavors marinate and leads to a sturdier burger.

To cook, shape the mixture into patties. If you're not using a nonstick pan, then you may want to prepare the pan by brushing it with a tad of oil to avoid sticking. Place the patties in a pan on the stovetop over medium heat for 15 minutes on each side. Pans and stovetops vary, so begin to check the patties at 10 minutes. If you try to slide your spatula under a patty and it won't give, then it isn't ready and needs to cook longer.

You can also bake the patties on a parchment-lined cookie sheet at 375°F (191°C) for about 20 to 25 minutes on each side. Allow the patties to cool and set for 5 to 7 minutes. Serve on buns with the toppings of your choice.

Notes: Make sure you soak your chickpeas overnight or for at least 6 hours.

Any type of starchy potato works—I use red. Sweet potato is not recommended as it is not starchy enough. Cook the potato in the microwave or oven. I don't recommend boiling it because it makes the potato too wet.

Kids: Make patties into a smaller slider size or into nuggets. Serve sauce on the side as a dipper.

WANT S'MORE OF MY BURGER?

Who says burgers can't be dessert? There is nothing like a fudgy, chocolate-rich brownie. I love them dense and a tad undercooked. This dessert burger patty was pretty much nailed on the first try! I knew what I was looking for, and it did not disappoint. If you're a cakey brownie type of person, then perhaps check yourself, but really, I may convert you. Just as gooey and even more delicious, this s'mores-inspired dessert burger is perfect for kids (and adults) of all ages!

PATTY (SEE NOTE)

½ cup (50 g) oat flour

½ cup (56 g) cocoa powder
(I use Dutch processed)

¼ tsp baking powder

¼ tsp sea salt

½ cup (100 g) cooked kidney beans,
drained and rinsed (see notes)

1 cup (180 g) vegan chocolate chips,
divided

¼ cup (45 g) almond butter

¼ cup (60 ml) maple syrup

6 Medjool dates, pitted

2 tbsp (30 ml) full-fat canned
coconut milk

½ tsp vanilla extract

BUN

8 graham cracker squares
(4 rectangles cut in half)

80 mini vegan marshmallows,
10 for each rectangle

TOPPING

Mind-Blowing Chocolate Sauce
(page 164)

Preheat the oven to 375°F (191°C).

Place the flour, cocoa powder, baking powder and salt in a bowl and mix to incorporate.

Place the kidney beans, ½ cup (90 g) of chocolate chips, almond butter, maple syrup, dates, coconut milk and vanilla extract into a food processor, and blend well until perfectly smooth.

Add the dry ingredients, and blend again until everything is mixed.

Add the rest of the chocolate chips and pulse a few times to mix them in.

Using your hands, shape the mixture into 4 patties (you want each to fit on a graham cracker square), and place them on a parchment-lined cookie sheet.

Bake for 13 to 15 minutes until the outer edges begin to harden, and then remove them from oven. They will cook a bit more as they cool, and you don't want to overbake them.

Once done, place the graham crackers on a parchment-lined cookie sheet and top with about 10 mini marshmallows each. Bake for 5 to 8 minutes until the marshmallows begin to melt.

Remove them from the oven, and place a patty on each graham cracker piece. Top them with another graham cracker to make a sandwich. Drizzle chocolate sauce on top and devour.

Notes: This is heavy on the patty and light on the bun because chocolate should always take center stage.

Don't let the kidney beans throw you off—before I created this, I was not a fan of beans in my desserts but this converted me.

APPLE PIE GETS A FACE-LIFT

Just as good as traditional apple pie except you get it all to yourself! I took my favorite flavors, brought them up a notch and created this cinnamon apple extreme dessert. Eat it warm and take in the comfort. You may need stretchy pants for this one.

6 Medjool dates

1 cup (121 g) raw pecans

½ cup (80 g) oats (gluten-free if needed)

½ cup (96 g) coconut sugar (or other sugar of your choice)

1 tsp cinnamon

½ tsp sea salt

Coconut oil, for greasing pan

Sticky Almond Caramel, for topping (page 167)

PATTY

2 cups (360 g) peeled and chopped apples (about 2 apples, see note)

½ cup (118 ml) full-fat canned coconut milk

¼ cup (48 g) coconut sugar (or other sugar of your choice)

1 tsp cinnamon

Preheat the oven to 350°F (177°C).

Put the dates in a bowl of hot water and allow them to soak while you gather the other ingredients, about 5 minutes or so.

Once the dates are soft, remove the pits and put them in a food processor with the pecans, oats, coconut sugar, cinnamon and sea salt. Pulse until you get a doughlike consistency.

Prepare 8 of the cups in a muffin tin with a light coat of coconut oil to prevent sticking. Divide the dough evenly into 8 sections. Press down a bit to make a bowl-like shape. You don't want it too deep; just slight enough so that the apples don't all slide off the edge when you put them together. These will be your "buns."

Cover with foil and bake for 10 to 15 minutes. Bake for less time for a soft, chewy texture and longer for a crispier texture. Nuts can burn easily, so stop cooking when the edges begin to brown. You want to cook them just long enough so they stay together but don't get too crisp.

Meanwhile, place the apples, coconut milk, coconut sugar and cinnamon into a saucepot. Bring it to a boil. Reduce the heat to medium and cook, mixing well until the apples are soft, thicken and become sticky, about 5 to 8 minutes.

Once the buns are done, serve the apple mixture inside two buns with the caved-in sections facing inward toward the apples. Top with almond caramel!

Note: You can use any kind of apples you prefer, but a sweeter variety is recommended.

Burritos

Because anything wrapped in a tortilla is a win. As a San Diegan, Mexican food is woven into my everyday life. Even as a young kid from a family of immigrants, my mom created her own "burrito" (Yiayia's Greek Burrito on page 98!) which is still eagerly devoured by us all.

Burritos are easy to throw together and range in flavor. They are so versatile and can easily be filled with power-packed ingredients that make them a one-stop meal. They are a mom's savior when nothing else is planned because a simple trio of beans, rice and avocado can easily be a healthy meal your kids won't throw at you.

Burritos make "clean out the fridge" day easy, all you need is a little imagination and a few tortillas! If I could create a cooking show, I would make a version of *Chopped*, where the participants would be given a box of ingredients and they would have to find the most creative and delicious way possible to make them into burritos. If you're a TV network and reading this, I thought of it first! Perhaps you're still unsure? I challenge you to eat your way through this chapter without devouring every bite.

SWEET POTATO AND WHITE BEAN "SAUSAGE" BREAKFAST BURRITOS

Wake up to a hearty breakfast, because sometimes we need more than yogurt. Protein, healthy carbs, veggies . . . you really can't ask for more.

2 cups (400 g) cooked or canned white beans (such as great northern beans), drained and rinsed

2 tsp (1 g) dried oregano

2 tsp (1 g) dried thyme

1 tsp crushed fennel (see notes)

1 tsp garlic powder

1 to 1½ tsp red pepper flakes

¾ tsp sea salt

¾ tsp lemon pepper

SWEET POTATO HASH

¾ cup (114 g) chopped sweet or yellow onion

1 tsp sea salt

Low-sodium veggie broth (about ½ cup [118 ml]), divided, or drizzle of oil, for sautéing

1½ cups (270 g) chopped sweet potato

¾ cup (128 g) chopped bell peppers, any color or a mix

¼ cup (43 g) chopped spicy hot pepper of choice, optional (see notes)

1 tsp dried oregano

TO SERVE

Smoky Tangy Cream (page 135) or mix Healthy Vegan Mayo, WHAT? (page 147) with hot sauce

4 to 5 tortillas

Preheat the oven to 375°F (191°C). Coarsely chop the white beans either with a knife on a cutting board or pulse in a food processor. Make sure they are not too dry or the spices won't stick well. Put them in a bowl and add oregano, thyme, fennel, garlic powder, red pepper flakes, salt and lemon pepper. Mix well to incorporate the spices.

Spread the coated beans on a parchment-lined cookie sheet and bake for 20 minutes or until the outer edges begin to get crisp. Set it aside to cool. These are your "sausage" crumbles.

Meanwhile, to make the sweet potato hash, put the onions and salt in a medium-size pan with ¼ cup (60 ml) of the broth. Sauté over medium heat until the onions are beginning to brown and get fragrant, about 4 to 5 minutes. Add the sweet potato and remaining broth if needed, and cook for 5 to 7 minutes until the sweet potato is soft. Add the bell peppers, hot peppers, if using, and oregano, and continue to sauté until they're cooked through, about 5 to 8 minutes. If needed, add more broth.

Serve in tortillas with the toppings of your choice. To fold the burrito, fold the sides over toward the center, then roll upward to create a burrito. (See page 15 for step-by-step photos.) You can grill the seam for 7 to 8 minutes until it seals and closes the burrito. You can also grill the other side to make it crisp.

Notes: For the crushed fennel, I simply take regular fennel seed and crush it with the back of a spoon. This helps disperse the flavor better.

Any hot peppers or mix will work here (jalapeño, serrano, cherry bomb, poblano or anaheim). These are optional for added spice. If you don't use them, then add an additional ¼ cup (43 g) of bell peppers.

Kids: This can be served as a bowl if folding a burrito is too hard!

Yield: 4 TO 5 BURRITOS

Level: 2

CAULI HASH BROWN BREAKFAST POCKETS

Swap some of your regular potatoes with the low-carb lover alternative: cauliflower! With all the flavor of traditional hash browns, this power veggie mix makes it's sneak peek debut in this Mexican-inspired burrito. It's a perfect way to start your day.

1 cup (200 g) grated potato (red or russet works best, see notes)

1 cup (230 g) grated cauliflower (see notes)

¼ cup (38 g) finely chopped sweet or yellow onion

¼ cup (10 g) finely chopped cilantro

3 tbsp (18 g) almond flour (see notes)

½ tsp sea salt, divided

½ tsp garlic powder

¼ tsp ground black pepper

1½ cups (300 g) cooked or canned black beans, drained and rinsed

1½ cups (270 g) chopped avocado

World's Best Roasted Salsa (page 132)

4 to 5 tortillas

Hot sauce, optional but highly recommended

Preheat the oven to 400°F (204°C) degrees.

Place the potato in a colander and rinse well to get as much starch off as you can. Then place it in a towel and squeeze out as much water as possible.

Place the cauliflower, dried potato, onion, cilantro, almond flour, ¼ teaspoon of salt, garlic powder and pepper in a bowl, and mix until well combined.

Drop spoonfuls of the mixture onto a parchment-lined cookie sheet so they make haystack-looking piles that are somewhat stuck together. You should make between 18 and 20 stacks. Bake for 35 to 40 minutes or until brown and crispy on edges. Allow it to cool and set for 5 to 7 minutes.

Meanwhile, mix the black beans and avocado with the other ¼ teaspoon of salt and set aside.

Serve in tortillas with the toppings of your choice. To fold the burrito, fold the sides over toward the center, then roll upward to create a burrito. (See page 15 for step-by-step photos.) You can grill the seam for 7 to 8 minutes until it seals and closes the burrito. You can also grill the other side to make it crisp.

Notes: You can use the grater attachment on your food processor to quickly and easily shred the potato and cauliflower.

Substituting another flour isn't recommended; the almond flour adds some whole food–based fats into the hash browns, which helps give them a crisp texture and flavorful taste. However, if you do want to use regular flour, then you can add a small drizzle of oil to the mixture to help add an extra crispness to the outside.

Kids: Serve in a bowl if a burrito is too hard!

VEGGIE-PACKED PIZZA BURRITOS

Your favorite veggie pizza all rolled up into an easy-to-eat burrito! Baked to a perfect crisp, smothered in sauces and ready for you to dive right in. I think you want to be here when Italy meets Mexico!

4 to 5 tortillas

½ cup (65 g) sliced red onion

1 tsp sea salt

Low-sodium veggie broth (about ½ cup [118 ml]), divided, or drizzle of oil, for sautéing

2 tbsp (20 g) coarsely chopped garlic

1 cup (76 g) sliced mushrooms

1 cup (161 g) chopped zucchini (see note)

½ cup (85 g) chopped bell peppers, any color or a mix

Quick-and-Easy Pizza Sauce (page 152)

1 cup (40 g) chopped fresh spinach

Cream Sauce for the Soul (page 159)

White Bean "Sausage" Crumbles (from the Sweet Potato and White Bean "Sausage" Breakfast Burritos on page 77), optional

¼ cup (45 g) sliced olives

Preheat the oven to 350°F (177°C).

Set your tortillas out at room temperature or quickly warm them in the microwave.

While the tortillas are warming, place the red onion and salt in a medium-size pan with ¼ cup (60 ml) of the broth. Sauté over medium heat until the onion is beginning to brown and get fragrant, about 4 to 5 minutes. Add the garlic and sauté for about 1 to 2 minutes until the garlic is browned. Add the mushrooms, zucchini, bell peppers and the remaining broth if needed. Continue to sauté until everything is cooked through and the liquid has evaporated, about 5 to 7 minutes.

Once the veggies are cooked and the tortillas are warm, spread 2 to 3 tablespoons of (30 to 45 ml) pizza sauce in the middle of each tortilla. Add ¼ cup (10 g) of the fresh spinach over the sauce, and add ¼ of the sautéed veggie mixture over the spinach. Cover with 2 to 3 tablespoons (30 to 45 ml) cream sauce and olives. If you're using the White Bean "Sausage" Crumbles, add those now.

To fold the burrito, fold the sides over toward the center, then roll upward to create a burrito. (See page 15 for step-by-step photos.) You can grill the seam for 7 to 8 minutes until it seals and closes the burrito. You can also grill the other side to make it crisp.

Note: This burrito can easily be customized with the veggies of your choice. Just make sure the total amount is about the same so you have enough to fill your burritos.

Kids: This can be served as a bowl if folding a burrito is too hard!

BLACK BEAN AND PUMPKIN WET BURRITOS

I'm creating all the comfort food I can for you all. These burritos are so easy to throw together, but they leave you with a fancy feel. "Fake it 'til you make it" is a great mantra to have as you serve this one to your fam. The sweetness of the pumpkin complements the tang of the chiles and touch of spice well. Get ready for a meal that will warm you up from the inside out.

1½ cups (300 g) cooked black beans, drained and rinsed

1 cup (40 g) chopped fresh spinach

1 cup (180 g) canned pumpkin (see notes)

½ cup (72 g) cooked frozen (defrosted to room temp) or fresh corn

½ cup (25 g) sliced green onions

1 (4-oz [28-g]) can diced mild green chiles

1 tsp chili powder

1 tsp garlic powder

1 tsp onion powder

½ to 1 tsp chipotle powder, optional

¾ tsp sea salt

Cream Sauce for the Soul (page 159), optional (see notes)

No-Cook Enchilada Sauce (page 155)

TO SERVE

4 to 5 tortillas

Sliced green onions

Fresh cilantro

Preheat the oven to 350°F (177°C).

Mix the beans, spinach, pumpkin, corn, green onions, chiles, chili powder, garlic powder, onion powder, chipotle powder and salt in a large bowl.

Split the filling among the tortillas, and drizzle some cream sauce, if using, over the filling.

To fold the burrito, fold the sides over toward the center and above the filling, then roll upward to create a burrito. (See page 15 for step-by-step photos.) Place the burritos on a parchment-lined baking sheet and bake for about 20 minutes or until they're crisp. Carefully flip them over using a spatula and bake for 5 minutes until they're crisp on the other side.

Remove the burritos from the oven, and top them with enchilada sauce. Sprinkle the green onions and cilantro if desired (either before or after baking again). Bake for 5 to 7 minutes until the sauce is hot. Serve immediately! You can also wait to top with sauces until right before eating, but you may need a few extra minutes for the burritos to heat throughout.

Notes: If you prefer to use freshly cooked pumpkin, you can, but note that it is different in texture so you may want to purée it well before using. It is also a bit wetter, so the burrito filling will not be as thick and may be runny.

If you want to keep this really easy, then you can leave out the cream sauce. It adds another layer of flavor, but the burrito is still good without it.

Kids: Leave out the chipotle powder. This can be served as a bowl if folding a burrito is too hard!

Yield: 4 TO 5
BURRITOS

Level: 1

CHIPOTLE AND LIME FOREVER

Chipotle and lime were meant to be soul mates. The flavor combo is insanely amazing. This easy-to-throw-together burrito is meant to be eaten in silence. The flavor gods need to be thanked for this one.

1 cup (170 g) chopped red, yellow and green bell pepper mix

½ cup (85 g) chopped spicy pepper of choice (jalapeño, cherry bomb, etc.)

½ cup (76 g) chopped red onion

Low-sodium veggie broth (about ½ cup [118 ml]) or drizzle of oil, for sautéing

1 tsp sea salt

1 tsp garlic powder

2 tbsp (30 ml) fresh lime juice

RICE AND BEANS

1½ cups (241 g) cooked brown rice

1 cup (200 g) cooked or canned black beans, drained and rinsed

¼ cup (10 g) chopped fresh cilantro

1 tbsp (15 ml) fresh lime juice

¾ tsp sea salt

½ tsp chipotle powder

TO SERVE

4 to 5 tortillas

Avocado

Shredded cabbage

Smoky Tangy Cream (page 135) or World's Best Roasted Salsa (page 132)

Sauté the peppers and onion in a pan over medium heat with veggie broth, salt, garlic powder and lime juice until cooked and fragrant, about 10 to 12 minutes. You may need to add more broth if it gets too dry. The mixture is ready when the veggies are soft and almost sticky looking.

To make the rice and beans, put the cooked rice, beans, cilantro, lime juice, salt and chipotle powder in a bowl and mix well.

Once everything is ready, build the burritos by filling the tortillas with the rice and beans, sautéed veggies, avocado and shredded cabbage.

Drizzle the sauce or salsa over the filling ingredients.

To fold the burrito, fold the sides over toward the center, then roll upward to create a burrito. (See page 15 for step-by-step photos.) You can grill the seam for 7 to 8 minutes until it seals and closes the burrito. You can also grill the other side to make it crisp.

Kids: This can be served as a bowl if folding a burrito is too hard! Do not add spicy peppers or chipotle powder. Substitute spicy peppers with bell peppers.

MY BIG FAT GREEK BURRITO

This burrito may be simple, but it packs a lot of traditional flavor. The fresh crisp ingredients in the salad give that perfect mix of textures. And the orzo helps fill you up and keeps you satisfied. One of my favorite carbs as a kid, and still now as an adult, orzo needed to make an appearance somewhere.

ORZO SALAD

1 cup (125 g) cooked orzo (gluten-free if needed)

6 tbsp (60 g) chopped tomatoes

6 tbsp (57 g) chopped cucumber

2 tbsp (19 g) chopped red onion

1 tsp dried oregano

¾ tsp sea salt

¼ tsp ground black pepper

1 tsp lemon juice

BEAN FILLING

2 cups (400 g) cooked or canned chickpeas, drained and rinsed

6 tsp (3 g) dried oregano

3 tsp (2 g) dried thyme

1 tsp sea salt

½ tsp ground black pepper

3 tbsp (23 g) Yiayia's Authentic Tzatziki (page 160)

TO SERVE

4 to 5 tortillas

Yiayia's Authentic Tzatziki (page 160)

Lettuce

Mix the cooked orzo in a bowl with the tomatoes, cucumber, red onion, oregano, salt, pepper and lemon juice. Set it aside.

In another bowl, use a fork to mash the chickpeas, oregano, thyme, salt, pepper and Yiayia's Authentic Tzatziki.

Serve in tortillas with the toppings of your choice. To fold the burrito, fold the sides over toward the center, then roll upward to create a burrito. (See page 15 for step-by-step photos.) You can grill the seam for 7 to 8 minutes until it seals and closes the burrito. You can also grill the other side to make it crisp.

Kids: This can be served as a bowl if folding a burrito is too hard!

IT'S GAME TIME

Save time and eat your chips and dip all in one roll! It's a little like an onion dip pocket. This burrito just screams game time, whether it's football or soccer, or even just the game of how fast you can devour this. The savory onion and garlic flavor is so good, you'll have trouble knowing when to stop.

1 cup (110 g) raw cashews

2 cups (400 g) cooked or canned white beans (such as great northern beans), drained and rinsed

1 cup (22 g) crushed potato chips

¼ cup (50 g) minced onion flakes

1 tbsp (8 g) onion powder

2 tsp (1 g) dried parsley

1 tsp garlic powder

1 tsp sea salt

½ tsp celery seed

TO SERVE

4 to 5 tortillas

Red onion slices

Thinly sliced or shaved carrots

Ultimate Onion Dip (page 140)

Potato chips

Lettuce

Preheat the oven to 375°F (191°C).

Pulse the cashews in a food processor until they are in large crumbles.

Add in the beans, potato chips, onion flakes, onion powder, parsley, garlic powder, salt and celery seed, and pulse until you have large chunks. Do not overpulse or it will become puréed.

Lay out the mixture on a parchment-lined cookie sheet and bake for 15 to 20 minutes until the edges begin to brown. You want them warm but not crispy.

Meanwhile, assemble the toppings of your choice. Once the crumble is done, fill the burritos.

To fold the burrito, fold the sides over toward the center, then roll upward to create a burrito. (See page 15 for step-by-step photos.) You can grill the seam for 7 to 8 minutes until it seals and closes the burrito. You can also grill the other side to make it crisp.

Note: You can eat this as a warm or cold burrito.

Kids: This can be served as a bowl if folding a burrito is too hard!

FRITO PIE POUCHES

Imagine if your favorite indulgences were actually healthy . . . oh wait, this is! This burrito has rich comfort food written all over it. Spicy chili, warm roasted tomatoes and the sweet and smoky flavors of Tex-Mex all wrapped up in a perfect little package. Get ready for goodness.

¼ cup (50 g) dried chickpeas, soaked overnight (see notes)

½ cup (76 g) chopped sweet or yellow onion

Low-sodium veggie broth (about 1½ cups [358 ml]) or drizzle of oil, for sautéing

¾ tsp sea salt, divided

1 medium-size clove garlic, chopped

¼ cup (40 g) canned fire-roasted tomatoes

1 (4-oz [114-g]) can diced mild green chiles

1½ tbsp (12 g) chili powder

1 tbsp (8 g) cumin

1½ tsp (4 g) smoked paprika

1 tsp dried oregano

1½ tsp (7 ml) maple syrup

½ cup (100 g) cooked or canned kidney beans, drained and rinsed

½ cup (100 g) cooked or canned pinto beans, drained and rinsed

TO SERVE

5 tortillas

Chopped red onion

Shredded lettuce

Chopped tomatoes

THE Vegan Sour Cream (page 144)

Corn chips

Mild jalapeño slices

Add the soaked chickpeas to a food processor and process until they resemble a crumbled texture. Sauté the onion in a pan over medium heat with ½ cup (118 ml) of veggie broth and salt until it begins to get soft, about 4 to 5 minutes. Add the garlic and sauté for about 1 to 2 minutes until the garlic is browned. Add the chopped chickpeas and sauté for 1 to 2 minutes until they begin to dry, then add 1 cup (240 ml) of broth, tomatoes, chiles, chili powder, cumin, paprika, oregano, maple syrup and salt.

Cook over low heat for about 20 to 25 minutes until the chickpeas are cooked and the liquid has mostly evaporated. Watch closely, stir frequently and lower the heat if it begins to stick, which can happen if you are not using oil. Once the liquid is almost gone and the mixture is nice and thick, add the kidney and pinto beans.

Serve in tortillas with the toppings of your choice. To fold the burrito, fold the sides over toward the center, then roll upward to create a burrito. (See page 15 for step-by-step photos.) You can grill the seam for 7 to 8 minutes until it seals and closes the burrito. You can also grill the other side to make it crisp.

Notes: Make sure you soak your chickpeas overnight or for at least 6 hours.

Make a double batch of the filling and eat it again on the second day as a chili bowl!

Kids: This can be served as a bowl if folding a burrito is too hard!

CRISPY BUFFALO BRINGS THE HEAT

These little crispy bites of buffalo heaven may or may not make it to the wrap-and-serve stage. They give a hint of popcorn shrimp with their texture and ease of throwing them in your mouth, but try your best not to knock them all back. The end result will be a hit with both veggie and meat eaters.

2 cups (460 g) cauliflower, chopped in bite-size pieces

1 cup (200 g) cooked or canned white beans (such as great northern beans), drained and rinsed (reserve the liquid)

½ cup (118 ml) buffalo cayenne pepper hot sauce (I like Frank's Red Hot Buffalo Wings Sauce), plus extra to drizzle after baking

¼ cup (60 ml) liquid from the can of white beans (see notes)

½ cup (85 g) cornmeal

½ cup (30 g) bread crumbs (gluten-free if needed)

¼ cup (40 g) hemp seeds (see notes)

1 tbsp (2 g) dried parsley

1 tbsp (8 g) garlic powder

TO SERVE

4 to 5 tortillas

Vegan Ranch—The Real Deal (page 131)

Buffalo cayenne pepper hot sauce

Thinly sliced red onion

Shredded carrots

Sliced celery

Lettuce

Preheat the oven to 450°F (232°C). Place the cauliflower pieces, white beans, hot sauce and white bean liquid in a plastic bag or bowl and mix well to combine. Set the mixture aside to marinate and absorb while you prep the coating.

Place the cornmeal, bread crumbs, hemp seeds, parsley and garlic powder in a food processor and blend until everything is well mixed and chopped. You can also use a blender but it may not chop the hemp seeds as well. Place the mixture in another plastic bag or large bowl.

Using your hand or a slotted spoon, remove the cauliflower and beans from the marinade mix and add them to the crispy coating. Shake or mix well to coat. I like doing this in a baggie best because you can seal and firmly shake the bag to fully coat everything.

Spread the cauliflower evenly on a parchment-lined cookie sheet and bake for 25 minutes. Remove it from the oven and drizzle some more hot sauce on top of the cauliflower pieces. I use about ¼ cup (60 ml), but you can add as much or as little as you want. Put it back in the oven and bake for 5 to 10 minutes, depending on how crisp you prefer the cauliflower to be. Allow it to cool and set for 5 to 7 minutes.

Serve in tortillas with the toppings of your choice. To fold the burrito, fold the sides over toward the center, then roll upward to create a burrito. (See page 15 for step-by-step photos.) You can grill the seam for 7 to 8 minutes until it seals and closes the burrito. You can also grill the other side to make it crisp.

Notes: The liquid from the can of white beans is also known as aquafaba. It helps coat things so that the dry ingredients will stick better and gives them a nice crisp when baked. You can also add a small drizzle of oil here if you want.

A regular flour instead of hemp seeds would work in a pinch but because of the lack of fat, this may not crisp up as much, so a touch of oil would be recommended in this case.

Kids: This may be too spicy for kids.

CRAB CAKE PO' BOY

What do you get when you sprinkle a vegan crab cake with a po' boy, and then take it on vacation in Mexico? An amazing burrito you won't be able to put down! It's a touch of tang meets creamy, underlined by a spicy sweetness. Because it never gets boring around here.

½ cup (25 g) chopped green onion

½ cup (76 g) chopped celery

½ cup (85 g) chopped red pepper

1 (14-oz [397-g]) can artichoke hearts (see note)

¾ cup (151 g) cooked or canned white beans (such as great northern beans), drained and rinsed

1 tbsp (3 g) fresh chopped parsley

1 tsp sea salt

¼ tsp ground black pepper

1 cup (60 g) bread crumbs (gluten-free if needed)

2 tbsp (28 g) Tartar Sauce Extreme (page 139)

1 tbsp (15 ml) lemon juice

1 tbsp (15 ml) spicy brown or Dijon mustard

2 tsp (1 g) crushed red pepper flakes, optional

TO SERVE

4 to 5 tortillas

Shredded lettuce

Fresh tomatoes

Tartar Sauce Extreme (page 139)

Hot sauce

Paprika

Add the green onion, celery, red pepper and artichoke hearts to a food processor. Pulse until everything is chopped. Do not overmix; you want some larger pieces. Put the mixture into a bowl.

Next add the beans, parsley, salt and pepper into the processor and pulse only a few times, around 3 to 4. Don't overpulse or you will get hummus. Put the mixture in the bowl with the artichoke heart mix.

Using a spatula, fold in the bread crumbs, tartar sauce, lemon juice, mustard and optional red pepper flakes. Carefully mix to incorporate all of the ingredients, but don't overmix.

Put the mixture in the fridge for at least 20 minutes, an hour is best. Making this the day before and letting it sit overnight is optimal. This helps all flavors marinate.

Preheat the oven to 350°F (177°C).

Pour the mixture onto a parchment-lined cookie sheet, spreading it out but leaving pieces in chunks. Bake for 15 minutes or until the edges begin to crisp. Allow it to cool.

Serve in tortillas with the toppings of your choice. To fold the burrito, fold the sides over toward the center, then roll upward to create a burrito. (See page 15 for step-by-step photos.) You can grill the seam for 7 to 8 minutes until it seals and closes the burrito. You can also grill the other side to make it crisp.

Note: You want the artichoke hearts to have as little liquid as possible. To get them nice and dry, squeeze the liquid out with your hands, then wrap them in a paper towel and squeeze out more liquid until they're pretty dry.

Kids: This can be served as a bowl if folding a burrito is too hard! Leave out the crushed red pepper and hot sauce.

FALL HARVEST

So many flavors coming together in one recipe! You're going to need to cleanse your palate for this one. It's kind of like your mouth decided to harvest all the fall flavors at one time. I'm talking savory, sweet, tangy; it just doesn't stop. Get ready for a rich, warm and comforting meal.

THYME RICE

1 cup (210 g) uncooked brown rice (see notes)

1¾ cups (414 ml) low-sodium veggie broth (see notes)

1 tbsp (2 g) dried thyme

¾ tsp sea salt (see notes)

VEGGIE BAKE

2 cups (360 g) chopped butternut squash

½ cup (120 g) chopped shallots

¾ tsp sea salt

Low-sodium veggie broth (about ½ cup [118 ml]) or drizzle of oil, plus more for roasting

3 cups (1 kg) shaved or sliced Brussels sprouts, divided

1 cup (180 g) peeled and chopped apples

¼ cup (28 g) pistachios

RASPBERRY MAYO

½ cup (118 ml) Healthy Vegan Mayo, WHAT? (page 147)

2 tbsp (30 g) raspberry jelly or jam

TO SERVE

4 to 5 tortillas

Raspberry Mayo

Preheat the oven to 400°F (204°C).

Place the rice, broth, thyme and salt in a small pot and mix well. Bring it to a rapid boil. Reduce the heat, cover and simmer for about 30 minutes or until the liquid has evaporated. Remove the pot from the heat, let it stand for 5 minutes and then fluff the rice with a fork.

Mix together the butternut squash, shallots, salt and broth, and bake for about 15 minutes. Remove it from the oven and add 2 cups (680 g) of Brussels sprouts, apples, pistachios and the rest of the broth if needed. Using a spatula, mix everything together well. Bake it for 30 minutes or until the squash is browning at the edges. When it's done, put it into a bowl with the reserved cup (340 g) of raw shaved brussels sprouts and mix well.

While the veggie bake is cooking, make the raspberry mayo by mixing the mayo and raspberry jelly together in a small bowl. Set it aside for serving.

Serve in tortillas with raspberry mayo. To fold the burrito, fold the sides over toward the center, then roll upward to create a burrito. (See page 15 for step-by-step photos.) You can grill the seam for 7 to 8 minutes until it seals and closes the burrito. You can also grill the other side to make it crisp.

Notes: I like my rice on the al dente side, so when cooking you may need to add another ¼ cup (60 ml) of broth and cook for an extra 5 minutes if you prefer it well done. The rice isn't overly salty. The other parts of this burrito have plenty of salt, so I keep the rice on the milder side.

You can use water instead of broth for the rice, but the broth adds great flavor.

You may need to adjust the amount of salt if you don't use broth.

Kids: This can be served as a bowl if folding a burrito is too hard!

YIAYIA'S GREEK BURRITO

A very nontraditional meal resurrected from my Greeklish (Greek/English) childhood. Don't expect traditional Greek flavors here, simply my mom's (yiayia's) version of feeding us Mexican food when we were kids. She actually called it a taco, mostly because I think anything Mexican was a taco to us Greeks. Every bite brings back amazing memories even through this meatless version. The blue toothpicks are mild and the red are spicy. Choose carefully!

¼ cup (50 g) dried chickpeas, soaked overnight (see notes)

¼ cup (30 g) chopped walnuts, soaked overnight

¼ cup (50 g) dried brown or green lentils

Drizzle of oil, optional

1¾ cups (414 ml) low-sodium veggie broth

1 tbsp (15 ml) tomato sauce

1 to 3 tsp (5 to 15 ml) hot sauce (see notes), plus more for serving

½ to ¾ tsp sea salt (see notes)

¼ tsp ground black pepper

4 tortillas

1 cup (40 g) chopped lettuce

½ cup (80 g) chopped tomatoes

4 tbsp (38 g) chopped red onion

Preheat the oven to 350°F (177°C).

Coarsely chop the chickpeas, walnuts and lentils in a food processor. Be careful not to overchop. Add them to a medium-size pan. If you are using oil, sauté the bean mixture over medium-low heat with a drizzle of oil until it's coated, about 1 to 2 minutes. Add the broth, tomato sauce, hot sauce, salt and pepper. Cook partially covered over medium-low heat for about 20 to 25 minutes until the beans are cooked and the liquid has mostly evaporated. Watch closely, stirring frequently, and lower the heat if it begins to stick, which can happen if you are not using oil. Uncover when most of the liquid has evaporated, and continue to cook, stirring frequently until the liquid is almost gone. Set the pan aside to cool.

Fill tortillas in the center with the meaty bean/nut mixture, lettuce, tomatoes, red onion and hot sauce, if using. Simply fold the burrito by folding the sides over toward the center and secure them with a toothpick, blue for mild and red for spicy. See complete instructions on page 15. Place them on a parchment-lined cookie sheet and bake for about 20 minutes or until they're crisp. Serve immediately.

Notes: Make sure you soak your chickpeas overnight or for at least 6 hours.

Adjust the hot sauce to your liking. You can also take it out and add more tomato sauce instead to keep the burrito spice-free.

The hotter the hot sauce you use, the less salt you will need, so make sure to account for that.

Kids: This can be served as a bowl if folding a burrito is too hard! Reduce the hot sauce or don't use it altogether.

TANGY CURRIED CAULIFLOWER BURRITO

Curry isn't for everyone, me included, but with some tangy lime and fresh cilantro, it makes for a winning combo that even I would enjoy. I'm definitely on the low side of the curry powder chain, but ramp it up to really push that rich, spicy flavor through. Plus, after roasting with these awesome veggies, there's no way you'll be able to stop eating them!

1½ cups (344 g) chopped cauliflower

1 cup (240 g) chopped sweet potato

½ cup (76 g) sliced sweet or yellow onion

2 tbsp (30 ml) fresh lime juice

2 to 4 tsp (5 to 10 g) curry powder, to taste

1 tsp sea salt (see notes)

Low-sodium veggie broth (about 1¾ cups [414 ml]), divided (see notes)

½ cup (90 g) chopped zucchini

QUINOA

1 cup (185 g) uncooked quinoa

¼ cup (10 g) chopped fresh cilantro

2 to 4 tsp (5 to 10 g) curry powder, to taste

½ tsp garlic powder

½ tsp sea salt

1 tbsp (15 ml) fresh lime juice

TO SERVE

4 to 5 tortillas

Lettuce

Low-Fat Creamy Curry Sauce (page 136)

Preheat the oven to 450°F (232°C).

Combine the cauliflower, sweet potato, onion, lime juice, curry powder, salt and ¼ cup (60 ml) of broth in a bowl and mix well to coat. Put the mixture on a parchment-lined cookie sheet and bake for 15 minutes.

Add the zucchini to the cookie sheet, mix everything around to incorporate the zucchini and bake for 7 minutes until everything is nice and brown on the edges.

Meanwhile, put 1½ cups (355 ml) of broth, quinoa, cilantro, curry powder, garlic powder and salt in a small pot and mix well. Bring it to a rapid boil. Reduce the heat, cover and simmer for about 15 minutes or until the liquid has evaporated. Remove the pot from the heat, let it stand for 5 minutes, and then fluff the quinoa with a fork. Add the lime juice and mix well.

Serve on tortillas with lettuce and a drizzle of curry sauce. To fold the burrito, fold the sides over toward the center, then roll upward to create a burrito. (See page 15 for step-by-step photos.) You can grill the seam for 7 to 8 minutes until it seals and closes the burrito. You can also grill the other side to make it crisp.

Notes: You may need to adjust the amount of salt if you don't use broth.

You can use water instead of broth, but the broth adds great flavor.

Kids: This can be served as a bowl if folding a burrito is too hard!

FLAKY "FISH" BURRITO

This is my plant-based take on a fish burrito without using processed fake fish. The tang of the lemon and soft flaky cauliflower give both the flavor and texture you need. The creamy dill sauce is out-of-this-world amazing and makes the perfect complement for this unique combo!

1 cup (200 g) cooked or canned chickpeas, drained and rinsed (reserve the liquid)

1½ cups (344 g) cauliflower, chopped in bite-size pieces (a little less than half a small head)

6 tbsp (88 ml) liquid from the can of chickpeas (see notes)

1 tbsp (15 ml) lemon juice, plus more for serving

3 tbsp (18 g) almond flour (see notes)

3 tbsp (32 g) cornmeal

3 tbsp (11 g) bread crumbs

1½ tsp (8 g) sea salt

1½ tsp (1 g) dried parsley

1½ tsp (4 g) garlic powder

TO SERVE

4 to 5 tortillas

Creamy Dill with a Tangy Twist (page 151)

Hot sauce

Shredded cabbage

Preheat the oven to 450°F (232°C).

Using your hands, mash the chickpeas a little so that you have some big pieces. If the skins come off, feel free to discard them. This step is optional, but I prefer the texture of the final product when the chickpeas are a tad mashed.

Place the cauliflower and chickpeas in a bowl and mix well with the chickpea liquid and lemon juice.

In a baggie or another bowl, mix together the flour, cornmeal, bread crumbs, salt, parsley and garlic powder.

Using your hand or a slotted spoon, remove the cauliflower and chickpeas from the liquid mix and add them to the dry ingredients. Mix well to coat them. I like doing this in a baggie best because you can seal and firmly shake the bag to fully coat everything.

Spread the cauliflower and chickpeas evenly on a parchment-lined cookie sheet and bake for about 20 to 25 minutes, depending on how crisp you want it and how cooked you want the cauliflower. Allow it to cool and set for 5 to 7 minutes. Squeeze a bit more lemon juice on top for extra lemon flavor.

Serve in tortillas with the toppings of your choice. To fold the burrito, fold the sides over toward the center, then roll upward to create a burrito. (See page 15 for step-by-step photos.) You can grill the seam for 7 to 8 minutes until it seals and closes the burrito. You can also grill the other side to make it crisp.

Notes: The liquid from the can of chickpeas is also known as aquafaba. It helps coat things so that the dry ingredients will stick better and gives them a nice crisp when baked.

I use a fine-ground blanched almond flour, but because this isn't a baked good, any almond flour would work.

Kids: This can be served as a bowl if folding a burrito is too hard!

KINDA A SUSHI BURRITO

My love for Mexican food and sushi is strong, so it was only natural that this burrito would be the next step in our relationship. The mashed beans and spicy sauce make for the perfect protein boost. Add crispy sweet potato and all the delicious veggies, and you have a meal in a roll!

½ medium sweet potato, sliced into french fry–type strips

2 tbsp (30 ml) liquid from a can of white beans, or drizzle of oil (see notes)

1 cup (60 g) regular or panko bread crumbs (gluten-free if needed)

½ tsp sea salt

1½ cups (300 g) cooked or canned white beans (such as great northern beans), drained and rinsed (reserve the liquid)

½ cup (110 g) Healthy Vegan Mayo, WHAT? (page 147)

1 to 3 tsp (5 to 15 g) Sriracha or other hot sauce (depending on how spicy you want it)

2 cups (322 g) cooked sushi rice (see notes)

4 to 5 tortillas

1 avocado, sliced into strips

½ small yellow pepper, sliced into strips

½ small cucumber, sliced into strips

½ medium carrot, sliced into strips

8 to 10 asparagus spears

½ cup (20 g) pea sprouts

TO SERVE

Tamari or soy sauce

Preheat the oven to 450°F (232°C).

Put the sweet potato strips and bean liquid in a bowl and mix well to coat. In another bowl, mix the bread crumbs and salt.

Add the sweet potato strips to the bread crumb mixture a few at a time and coat them. The potatoes will be just slightly coated, not completely covered. This is okay, as you want just a slight crunch to them. If you want them fully enveloped in bread crumbs, you can coat first with the batter from the Buffalo Wing Sliders (page 63).

Place them on a parchment-lined cookie sheet and bake for 30 minutes or until they're crispy.

Meanwhile, mix the white beans, mayo and Sriracha in a small bowl using a fork to mash the beans. Keep it as chunky or make it as smooth as you like.

Once everything is ready, build the burritos by spreading the rice over the tortilla (you can dip your fingers in water to avoid getting sticky). Next spread the bean mixture over the rice. Place a few strips of crispy sweet potatoes, avocado, pepper, cucumber, carrot, asparagus and pea sprouts to cover the bean mixture, spreading them out evenly.

To fold the burrito, fold the sides over toward the center, then roll upward to create a burrito. (See page 15 for step-by-step photos.) You can grill the seam for 7 to 8 minutes until it seals and closes the burrito. You can also grill the other side to make it crisp.

Notes: The liquid from the can of white beans is also known as aquafaba. It helps coat things so that the dry ingredients will stick better and gives them a nice crisp when baked. You can also substitute with oil.

If you don't have or can't find sushi rice, any other rice will work.

Kids: Do not add Sriracha. This can be served as a bowl if folding a burrito is too hard!

ORIGINAL CALIFORNIA BURRITO

Being a Californian, I had to create a true California burrito. The challenge wasn't easy, considering meat is usually the center of this local favorite. But using my creativity to flavor and bake the beans in typical carne asada spices hit the nail on the head. Keeping it traditionally simple with some fries and guac makes this the first vegan whole food–based California burrito I've seen!

FRIJOLES ASADA

1¾ cups (352 g) cooked or canned black beans, drained and rinsed

1¾ cups (352 g) cooked or canned pinto beans, drained and rinsed

¼ cup (10 g) fresh chopped cilantro

1 tbsp (6 g) oat flour

1½ tsp (4 g) cumin

1½ tsp (4 g) chili powder

1½ tsp (1 g) dried oregano

¾ tsp garlic powder

¾ tsp sea salt (see notes)

¼ tsp white pepper (see notes)

GUACAMOLE

2 avocados

½ to 1 tsp fresh lime juice, to taste

¼ tsp sea salt

Dash of ground black pepper

TO SERVE

4 to 5 tortillas

Taters and Herbs (page 171, see notes)

Hot sauce

Preheat the oven to 375°F (191°C).

To make the frijoles asada, put the black beans, pinto beans, cilantro, oat flour, cumin, chili powder, oregano, garlic powder, salt and pepper in a food processor, and pulse a few times until you have large chunks. You simply want the beans chopped a bit. Do not overpulse or it will become puréed.

Spread the beans in an even thin layer on a parchment-lined cookie sheet and bake for 25 to 30 minutes, depending on how crisp you want them.

To make the guacamole, mash the avocados with lime juice, salt and pepper. Allow it to set for a few minutes for the flavors to mix in.

Fill the tortillas with the frijoles asada. Add the fries and guacamole, and top with hot sauce. To fold the burrito, fold the sides over toward the center, then roll upward to create a burrito. (See page 15 for step-by-step photos.) You can grill the seam for 7 to 8 minutes until it seals and closes the burrito. You can also grill the other side to make it crisp.

Notes: Adjust the salt depending on the amount in the beans you use and if you add hot sauce. The other parts of this recipe have plenty of salt, so you may be okay keeping the beans lower in salt content.

If you don't have white pepper, you can substitute black.

You will have plenty of fries to serve some on the side as well if you make the full recipe. You can also halve the Taters and Herbs recipe to have just enough for the burritos, but I wouldn't suggest it.

Kids: This can be served as a bowl if folding a burrito is too hard! Leave out the hot sauce.

QUINOA AND SAUTÉED VEGGIE BURRITO

Sometimes a simple seasoned sautéed veggie mix is all you need to satisfy your appetite. I mastered the art of cooking quinoa with that just-perfect al dente texture while creating these, and it pairs with the veggies like peanut butter and jelly.

QUINOA

1¼ cups (296 ml) low-sodium veggie broth (see notes)

1 cup (185 g) uncooked quinoa

¼ cup (40 g) World's Best Roasted Salsa (page 132)

1 tsp smoked paprika

½ tsp garlic powder

½ tsp sea salt (see notes)

VEGGIE SAUTE

¼ cup (38 g) chopped red onion

¾ to 1 cup (177 to 240 ml) veggie broth, divided, or drizzle of oil, for sautéing

¾ tsp sea salt, divided

1 tbsp (10 g) chopped fresh garlic

½ cup (120 g) chopped sweet potato

2 tbsp (21 g) chopped spicy pepper of choice (like jalapeño, cherry bomb, serrano)

½ cup (38 g) chopped mushrooms

½ cup (78 g) chopped zucchini

½ cup (20 g) freshly chopped cilantro

¼ cup (13 g) sliced green onions

TO SERVE

4 to 5 tortillas

Lettuce

THE Vegan Sour Cream (page 144)

To make the quinoa, put the broth, quinoa, salsa, paprika, garlic powder and salt in a small pot and mix well. Bring it to a rapid boil. Reduce the heat, cover and simmer for about 15 minutes or until the liquid has evaporated. Remove the pot from the heat, let it stand for 5 minutes, and then fluff the quinoa with a fork.

Meanwhile, sauté the onion in a pan over medium heat with ¼ cup (60 ml) of veggie broth and ¼ teaspoon of salt until it begins to soften, about 4 to 5 minutes. Add the garlic and sauté for about 1 to 2 minutes until the garlic is browned. Add the sweet potatoes and pepper and ¼ cup (60 ml) of broth, and sauté until the potatoes begin to soften, about 10 minutes. Add another ¼ to ½ cup (60 to 118 ml) of broth, and then add the mushrooms, zucchini, cilantro, green onions and ½ teaspoon of salt, and continue to cook until everything is soft, about 5 to 10 minutes depending on how al dente you like your zucchini.

Serve on tortillas with lettuce and a drizzle of sour cream. To fold the burrito, fold the sides over toward the center, then roll upward to create a burrito. (See page 15 for step-by-step photos.) You can grill the seam for 7 to 8 minutes until it seals and closes the burrito. You can also grill the other side to make it crisp.

Notes: You can use water instead of broth, but the broth adds great flavor.

You may need to adjust the amount of salt if you don't use broth.

Kids: This can be served as a bowl if folding a burrito is too hard! Leave out the spicy pepper.

SMOKY SPANISH GOODNESS

As my first burrito recipe created for this book, this holds a special place in my heart. The combination of sticky, sweet sautéed veggies with roasted salsa–flavored rice, savory black beans and the Smoky Tangy Cream (page 135) it's smothered in has me drooling just typing this.

RICE

1⅛ cups (266 ml) low-sodium veggie broth (see notes)

¾ cup (158 g) uncooked brown rice

6 tbsp (60 g) World's Best Roasted Salsa (page 132)

½ tsp sea salt, optional (see notes)

VEGGIE MIX

½ red pepper, thinly sliced

½ green pepper, thinly sliced

½ red onion, thinly sliced

Low-sodium veggie broth (about ½ cup [118 ml]), divided, or drizzle of oil, for sautéing

1 tsp sea salt

BEANS

2 cups (400 g) cooked or canned black beans, drained and rinsed (reserve the liquid)

¼ cup (60 ml) liquid from the can of black beans

1½ tsp (4 g) smoked paprika

¾ tsp garlic powder

¾ tsp cumin

¾ tsp oregano

½ tsp sea salt (see notes)

¼ tsp coriander

¼ to ½ tsp chipotle seasoning, optional

TO SERVE

Smoky Tangy Cream (page 135)

4 to 5 tortillas

Put the broth, rice, salsa and salt (if using) into a small pot and bring it to a boil. Turn the heat to medium-low and cook covered for 35 to 40 minutes, depending on how al dente you like your rice. Add an extra ¼ cup (60 ml) of broth if needed. Once done, turn off the heat and let it stand covered for 5 minutes. Fluff it with a fork. While the rice is cooking, make the other burrito parts.

To make the veggie mix, sauté the peppers and onion in a pan over medium-low heat with broth and salt until they're brown and caramelized, about 8 to 10 minutes. The mixture is ready when the veggies are soft and almost sticky looking.

To make the beans, put the beans, bean liquid, paprika, garlic powder, cumin, oregano, salt, coriander and chipotle seasoning, if using, in a small pot, mix well and cook over medium-low heat until it thickens, about 8 to 10 minutes.

Once everything is ready, build the burritos by topping each tortilla with rice, beans and sautéed veggies. Drizzle the Smoky Tangy Cream over the filling ingredients. To fold the burrito, fold the sides over toward the center, then roll upward to create a burrito. (See page 15 for step-by-step photos.) You can grill the seam for 7 to 8 minutes until it seals and closes the burrito. You can also grill the other side to make it crisp.

Notes: You can use water instead of broth, but the broth adds great flavor.

You may need to adjust the amount of salt in your rice if you don't use broth and also in your beans depending on how much salt your beans have.

Kids: Do not add chipotle seasoning. This can be served as a bowl if folding a burrito is too hard!

GARDEN DELIGHT

Using the natural flavors of delicious veggies to create a recipe is one of my favorite ways to show how good veggies can be. The savory mushrooms and sweetness of the caramelized red pepper make for an amazing combo, especially smothered in a fresh Basil Mayo. This is one burrito I was sad to see gone.

Low-sodium veggie broth (about ½ cup [118 ml]), divided

¼ cup (60 ml) tamari or soy sauce

1 tsp garlic powder

2 tbsp (30 ml) balsamic vinegar

4 portobello mushrooms, stems and gills removed and sliced into 5 to 6 pieces each

1 red pepper, sliced

¼ medium sweet or yellow onion, sliced

½ tsp sea salt

½ tsp smoked paprika

4 leaves swiss chard, stems removed

BASIL MAYO

½ cup (110 g) Healthy Vegan Mayo, WHAT? (page 147)

3 tbsp (8 g) chopped fresh basil

TO SERVE

4 tortillas

Tomatoes

Mix ¼ cup (60 ml) of broth, tamari, garlic powder and vinegar in a small bowl, and whisk well to make a marinade.

Place the mushrooms in a dish and pour the marinade over the top. Allow this to sit while preparing the other ingredients.

While the mushrooms are marinating, make the Basil Mayo. Mix the mayo with the basil in a small bowl until it's well incorporated. Set it aside for serving.

Sauté the pepper and onion in a pan over medium heat with ¼ cup (60 ml) of veggie broth and salt until they begin to soften, about 8 to 10 minutes. Add the mushrooms, remaining broth and paprika, and continue to sauté until everything is cooked through, about 10 to 12 minutes. If needed, add more broth or oil.

Make the burritos by placing a fresh chard leaf on a tortilla, then topping with the cooked veggie mix. The warmth of the layered vegetables will wilt the chard slightly. Add the fresh tomato and Basil Mayo.

To fold the burrito, fold the sides over toward the center, then roll upward to create a burrito. (See page 15 for step-by-step photos.) You can grill the seam for 7 to 8 minutes until it seals and closes the burrito. You can also grill the other side to make it crisp.

Kids: This can be served as a bowl if folding a burrito is too hard!

PAD THAI MEETS MEXICO

I love pad thai noodles with the same intensity I love burritos. So I figured, why not put them together? Throw in a little chickpea and peanut protein, load it up with veggies and of course a mouthwatering sauce, and you're all set for a perfect meal. You may want to eat this one alone, because nothing is worse than being bothered while in a food coma.

2 cups (180 g) cooked pad thai or brown rice noodles

Low-sodium veggie broth (about ½ cup [118 ml]), for sautéing, plus more for noodles

1 cup (200 g) cooked or canned chickpeas, drained and rinsed

¼ cup (40 g) chopped or crushed peanuts

2 tbsp (30 ml) Skinny Peanut Sauce (page 143)

1 medium red pepper, thinly sliced

1 large carrot, thinly sliced

1 medium zucchini, thinly sliced

¼ cup (60 ml) tamari or soy sauce

1 tbsp (15 ml) fresh lime juice

1 tsp sesame oil (omit if not using oil)

½ cup (25 g) sliced green onion

½ cup (20 g) chopped cilantro

2 cups (680 g) shredded cabbage

TO SERVE

4 to 5 tortillas

Skinny Peanut Sauce (page 143)

Mix the cooked noodles and a splash of broth in a bowl and set it aside.

Mash the chickpeas with your hands to create a bit of a crumble. Add the crushed peanuts and peanut sauce, and mix it well. Set it aside.

Sauté the pepper, carrot and zucchini in a pan over medium heat with tamari, lime juice, sesame oil and ½ cup (118 ml) of veggie broth until they begin to soften, about 8 to 10 minutes. Add the green onions and cilantro, and mix well. Cook for 2 to 3 more minutes until the onions and cilantro begin to wilt.

Once everything is ready, build the burritos by filling the tortillas with the noodles, bean and peanut mixture, sautéed veggies and shredded cabbage. Drizzle more peanut sauce over the filling ingredients. To fold the burrito, fold the sides over toward the center, then roll upward to create a burrito. (See page 15 for step-by-step photos.) You can grill the seam for 7 to 8 minutes until it seals and closes the burrito. You can also grill the other side to make it crisp.

Kids: This can be served as a bowl if folding a burrito is too hard!

LOW-CARB COLLARD LOVE

Looking for a low-carb way to satisfy your burrito needs? This is your guy: super flavorful and filling without the added heaviness of the tortilla. It's fresh and light, with a touch of warming spice. Sometimes it's good to go all green!

QUINOA

1¼ cups (296 ml) low-sodium veggie broth (see notes)

1 cup (185 g) uncooked quinoa

¼ cup (10 g) finely chopped cilantro

½ tsp chipotle powder

½ tsp sea salt (see notes)

FILLING

½ cup (76 g) chopped sweet or yellow onion

Low-sodium veggie broth (about ½ cup [118 ml]), divided, or drizzle of oil, for sautéing

½ tsp sea salt

1 tbsp (10 g) chopped garlic

¾ cup (128 g) chopped poblano pepper (see notes)

¾ cup (121 g) fire-roasted tomatoes

1½ cups (300 g) cooked or canned black beans, drained and rinsed

TO SERVE

4 to 5 collard leaves, stems removed

Smoky Tangy Cream (page 135)

To make the quinoa, put the broth, quinoa, cilantro, chipotle powder and salt in a small pot and mix well. Bring it to a rapid boil. Reduce the heat, cover and simmer for about 15 minutes or until the liquid has evaporated. Remove the pot from the heat, let it stand for 5 minutes and then fluff quinoa with a fork.

Meanwhile, sauté the onion in a pan over medium heat with ¼ cup (60 ml) veggie broth and salt until it begins to soften, about 4 to 5 minutes. Add the garlic and sauté for about 1 to 2 minutes until the garlic is browned. Add the peppers and the rest of the broth, and sauté until the peppers soften, about 5 to 7 minutes. Add the tomatoes and cook until some of the liquid has evaporated, just about 5 minutes. Add the beans and continue to cook for 5 minutes or so until the liquid is gone and the beans have warmed.

Serve on collard leaves (make sure to remove the stems), and top with a drizzle of Smoky Tangy Cream. To fold the burrito, fold the sides over toward the center, then roll upward to create a burrito. (See page 15 for step-by-step photos.)

Notes: You can use water instead of broth, but the broth adds great flavor.

You may need to adjust the amount of salt if you don't use the broth.

Make sure to remove the seeds from the peppers to avoid too much spice.

Kids: This can be served as a bowl if folding a burrito is too hard!

WRAPPED-UP CHILE RELLENOS

This is not your usual stuffed and fried poblano pepper! Roasted salsa, a meaty mixture of beans and nuts and a drizzle of a creamy sauce make a burrito best eaten with a knife and fork!

5 poblano peppers

¼ cup (50 g) dried chickpeas, soaked overnight

¼ cup (50 g) dried brown or green lentils

¼ cup (30 g) chopped walnuts, soaked overnight

½ cup (76 g) chopped sweet or yellow onion

Low-sodium veggie broth (about 2½ cups [592 ml]), divided

2 medium-size cloves garlic, chopped

½ cup (80 g) fire-roasted tomatoes

1 tbsp (8 g) cumin

1½ tsp (1 g) dried oregano

1¼ tsp (18 g) sea salt, divided

1 tsp chili powder

¼ tsp ground black pepper

5 tortillas

Cream Sauce for the Soul (page 159)

World's Best Roasted Salsa (page 132)

Sliced green onions

Fresh cilantro

Preheat the oven to broil. Place the poblano peppers on a foil-lined cookie sheet and broil on high for about 5 minutes until the exposed sides are blackened. Flip them over and broil for 5 minutes. Remove them from the oven and wrap the poblanos in the foil from the cookie sheet. Set them aside so they can steam while you make the filling.

Coarsely chop the chickpeas, lentils and walnuts in a food processor. Be careful not to overchop. Sauté the onion in a pan over medium heat with ½ cup (118 ml) of veggie broth and ¼ teaspoon of salt until it begins to soften, about 4 to 5 minutes. Add the garlic and sauté for about 1 to 2 minutes until the garlic is browned. Add the bean/nut mixture and sauté for 2 to 3 minutes until it begins to dry, then add 2 cups (480 ml) of broth, tomatoes, cumin, oregano, 1 teaspoon of salt, chili powder and pepper. Cook partially covered for about 20 to 25 minutes until the beans are cooked and the liquid has mostly evaporated. Stir frequently, and lower the heat if it begins to stick, which can happen if you are not using oil. Uncover when most of the liquid has evaporated and continue to cook, mixing frequently until the liquid is almost gone. Set aside.

Preheat the oven to 400°F (204°C). Remove the poblanos from the foil and carefully remove the skins. Gently cut a slit in each one, and remove the stem and seeds. Place each poblano on a tortilla opened and lying flat, put about one-fifth of the meaty bean/nut mixture and a spoonful of cream sauce in the pepper and then fold the pepper closed.

To fold the burrito, fold the sides over toward the center and above the stuffed poblano, then roll upward to create a burrito with the pepper stuffed inside. (See page 15 for step-by-step photos.) Place the burritos on a parchment-lined baking sheet and bake for about 20 minutes. Carefully flip them over using a spatula and bake for 5 minutes until they're crisp.

Remove them from the oven and top them with more cream sauce and the roasted salsa. Sprinkle them with green onions and cilantro if desired (either before or after baking again). Bake for 5 to 7 minutes until the sauces are hot. Serve immediately!

Kids: This can be served as a bowl if folding a burrito is too hard!

SOPH'S NINE LAYERS OF AMAZING

Quote from the husband: "This is so amazing, it tastes like Taco Bell." Now, whether a compliment or a testament to his bachelor days, I'm taking this and running with it. We've got crunchy chips topped with layer upon layer of flavor. It's like you're eating a seven-layer dip and chips all rolled into one handheld dinner. Don't skimp on the layers because it's worth every extra effort!

2 cups (43 g) tortilla chips

BEAN LAYER

2 cups (400 g) cooked or canned black beans, do not drain

3 tsp (8 g) cumin

3 tsp (8 g) onion powder

2 tsp (5 g) garlic powder

1½ tsp (1 g) dried oregano

¾ tsp sea salt (see note)

AVOCADO LAYER

1 avocado

¾ tsp lemon pepper

½ tsp sea salt

TO SERVE

4 tortillas

2 cups (680 g) shredded lettuce

¾ cup (121 g) World's Best Roasted Salsa (page 132)

¾ cup (90 g) THE Vegan Sour Cream (page 144)

½ cup (25 g) sliced green onions

½ cup (25 g) sliced black olives

½ cup (25 g) mild jalapeño slices

Lightly crush the tortilla chips and set them aside.

To make the bean layer, place the beans with liquid (do not drain), cumin, onion powder, garlic powder, oregano and salt into a small pot and heat it over medium heat on the stovetop. Bring it to a boil, lower the heat and simmer, stirring frequently until the beans thicken, about 8 to 10 minutes. They will thicken more as they cool. Mash the beans with a fork as you stir to get the beans to a refried-type consistency. You can also do this with a potato masher.

To make the avocado layer, combine the avocado, pepper and salt in a small bowl. Mash it with a fork to incorporate. Make it as smooth or chunky as you prefer.

To serve, layer each tortilla as follows: chips on the bottom, lettuce, beans, avocado, salsa, sour cream, green onions, black olives and jalapeño slices.

To fold the burrito, fold the sides over toward the center, then roll upward to create a burrito. (See page 15 for step-by-step photos.) You can grill the seam for 7 to 8 minutes until it seals and closes the burrito. You can also grill the other side to make it crisp.

Note: You may need to adjust the amount of salt depending on how much salt your beans have.

Kids: This can be served as a bowl if folding a burrito is too hard!

VEGGIE TIAN ALL ROLLED UP

This is a two-recipe-in-one kind of treat. Eat it burrito style or like a typical veggie tian (a layered baked vegetable dish)!

PARMNUTSAN

½ cup (50 g) almond flour

¼ cup (31 g) pine nuts

¼ to ½ tsp sea salt, to taste

¼ tsp garlic powder

⅛ tsp ground mustard seed

VEGGIE TIAN (SEE NOTE)

½ medium sweet or yellow onion, sliced in strips

Low-sodium veggie broth (about ¾ cup [177 ml]) or drizzle of oil, for sautéing and baking

¾ tsp sea salt

2 medium-size cloves garlic, chopped

2 cups (400 g) cooked or canned white beans (such as great northern beans), drained and rinsed

1 small red or russet potato (about 4 inches [10 cm] long), peeled and sliced into ⅛-inch (3-mm)-thick rounds

1 small eggplant, sliced into ¼-inch (6-mm)-thick rounds

1 small zucchini, sliced into ¼-inch (6-mm)-thick rounds

1 small yellow squash, sliced into ¼-inch (6-mm)-thick rounds

2 medium-size tomatoes, finely chopped

¼ cup (10 g) fresh chopped parsley

2 tsp (1 g) dried oregano

Fresh spinach leaves

5 tortillas

Preheat the oven to 400°F (204°C). Make the ParmNUTsan by putting the almond flour, pine nuts, salt, garlic powder and mustard seed into a food processor and blending until they're very finely chopped.

To make the veggie tian, sauté the onion in a pan over medium-low heat with ¼ cup (60 ml) of veggie broth and salt until it begins to brown and caramelize, about 8 to 10 minutes. Add more broth if needed. Add the garlic and sauté for about 1 to 2 minutes until the garlic is browned. Place this in the bottom of a 9 × 13-inch (23 × 33-cm) pan. Sprinkle the white beans on top.

Place the sliced potatoes, eggplant, zucchini and squash over the beans in a domino-like formation (not stacked on top of each other, but sides facing up so you can see each piece as you layer), alternating them until the rows fill the pan. You should be able to fit them all in.

Sprinkle the top with ½ cup (118 ml) of veggie broth, chopped tomatoes, chopped parsley, dried oregano and ½ cup (90 g) of the ParmNUTsan. Cover the pan with foil and bake for 30 minutes. Uncover and bake for 20 to 25 minutes until the top is golden brown and the vegetables are cooked.

Place spinach on each tortilla, then put some baked veggie tian on top of the spinach. The warmth of the layered vegetables will wilt the spinach slightly. Top with more ParmNUTsan. To fold the burrito, fold the sides over toward the center, then roll upward to create a burrito. (See page 15 for step-by-step photos.) You can grill the seam for 7 to 8 minutes until it seals and closes the burrito. You can also grill the other side to make it crisp.

Note: You can also substitute any of the veggies; just make sure the overall count is the same.

Kids: This can be served as a bowl if folding a burrito is too hard!

THE ULTIMATE MEXICAN CHURRO

Cinnamon and sugar is a mind-blowing combination, and the draw of those deep-fried churros is hard to resist. Now you can make them at home without the oil but all of the flavor! The only problem is you won't be able to stop eating them. Get ready for the sweet taste of heaven.

BATTER

1 cup (96 g) almond flour (see notes)

1 cup (240 ml) unsweetened plain cashew or almond milk

2 tbsp (24 g) coconut sugar

1 tsp cinnamon

COATING

¼ cup (48 g) coconut sugar

¼ cup (60 ml) evaporated cane juice or cane sugar

2 tbsp (12 g) almond flour (see notes)

1 tbsp (11 g) cornmeal

1 tbsp (8 g) cinnamon

¼ tsp sea salt

TO SERVE

4 tortillas (see notes)

Sticky Almond Caramel (page 167), to dip

Preheat the oven to 375°F (191°C).

Whisk the almond flour, milk, coconut sugar and cinnamon in a shallow dish to make the batter.

In another shallow dish, combine the coconut sugar, cane juice, almond flour, cornmeal, cinnamon and salt to make the coating.

Dip each tortilla in the batter, making sure both sides are covered, then place it in the coating. Tightly roll up the tortilla, then roll it well in coating and place it on a parchment-lined cookie sheet. Bake for 20 to 25 minutes, flip over each churro and bake for 5 or so minutes until they're crispy. Use the caramel sauce as a dip. Enjoy warm!

Notes: I use a fine-ground blanched almond flour, but because this isn't a baked good, any almond flour would work.

You want your tortillas to be as soft as possible for the best end result. Warm the tortillas by wrapping them in a damp paper towel and placing them in the microwave for 30 seconds. If they're not warm and soft, continue to microwave them at 15 second increments until they are. If you don't have a microwave, then steam them using a double boiler.

Yield: 4 BURRITOS		

FULLY LOADED "FRIED" BANANA SPLIT

It's two of my favorites all rolled into one. Crispy peanut butter–covered banana goodness paired with creamy ice cream, warm chocolate sauce and gooey caramel, and topped with crunchy nuts and colorful sprinkles. Hello indulgence!

1 cup (240 ml) unsweetened plain almond or cashew milk (see notes)

¾ cup (135 g) creamy peanut butter (see notes)

½ cup (48 g) almond flour (see notes)

¼ cup (48 g) coconut sugar

4 bananas

4 tortillas (see notes)

CRISPY COATING

1 cup (192 g) coconut sugar (or other sugar of choice)

8 graham cracker rectangles, crushed

TO SERVE

Mind-Blowing Chocolate Sauce (page 164)

Sticky Almond Caramel (page 167)

Your favorite vegan ice cream

Sliced fresh strawberries

Your favorite vegan whipped cream

Sprinkles

Chopped nuts of choice

Preheat the oven to 375°F (191°C).

Mix the milk, peanut butter, flour and coconut sugar in a shallow dish. Whisk well.

Put the coconut sugar and crushed graham crackers on a plate or shallow dish and mix to incorporate.

Peel the bananas and roll each in the batter, coating it well.

Then roll the bananas in the crispy coating. You can also place the bananas in the dish and use your hands or a spoon to coat them.

Place each banana on the edge of a tortilla and roll it up in the tortilla. Secure the tortilla edge with a bit of peanut butter to keep it closed. Roll the whole thing in the batter again and then in the crispy coating.

Put the burritos on a parchment-lined cookie sheet and bake for 20 to 25 minutes until they're crispy. Meanwhile, make the chocolate sauce and caramel if you haven't already.

Once the rolled bananas are done, allow them to cool a bit so you don't burn yourself. Serve with your favorite ice cream and toppings!

Notes: Make sure your milk and peanut butter are at room temperature. Placing your peanut butter out to warm to room temperature will make sure it gets really creamy. You can also warm it slightly in the microwave. This helps make sure that your batter won't seize up.

I use a fine-ground blanched almond flour, but because this isn't a baked good, any almond flour would work.

You want your tortillas to be as soft as possible for the best end result. Warm the tortillas by wrapping them in a damp paper towel and placing them in the microwave for 30 seconds. If they're not warm and soft, continue to microwave them at 15 second increments until they are. If you don't have a microwave, then steam them using a double boiler.

Sauces

Saucaholic: one who can't stop creating and eating sauces. A saucaholic does not want or need an intervention, especially one who creates sauces using all whole food ingredients.

Sauce queen isn't a bad nickname for someone like me. Sauces are life, the fuel for my madness. On top of bringing the flavor of recipes up two notches, at least, sauces like these can provide many nutrients to a meal. Whether you smother, dip or simply drink them, sauces should accompany every single meal. Mix and match them, get creative, bring these rainbows into your cloudy day. And when you come up for air, drop me a line to let me know you've joined my saucaholic nation.

VEGAN RANCH— THE REAL DEAL

Will the real ranch please stand up? Right here baby! A weekly staple used to get the littles, and some adults too, to eat their weight in veggies. You won't be able to stop dipping!

1 cup (240 ml) unsweetened plain cashew or almond milk

¼ cup plus 2 tsp (70 ml) white vinegar

5 tsp (25 ml) fresh lemon juice

1½ cups (167 g) raw cashews (see note)

1¼ tsp (6 g) sea salt

2 tsp (1 g) dried parsley

1 tsp garlic powder

1 tsp minced onion

½ tsp onion powder

½ tsp dried dill

¼ tsp ground black pepper

⅛ tsp mustard powder

Place the milk, vinegar and lemon juice in a bowl and allow it to sit while you assemble the rest of the ingredients.

Add the milk mixture, cashews and salt into a high-speed blender and purée until smooth.

Add the parsley, garlic powder, onion, onion powder, dill, black pepper and mustard powder to the blender and pulse until well mixed. Refrigerate the sauce to thicken.

Note: If you are not using a high-speed blender, there are a couple of options for making your sauce smooth: You can use a coffee grinder to grind everything to a fine powder, or make sure to soak your cashews overnight, or for at least 2 to 3 hours. If you forget, you can also boil them for 30 minutes.

WORLD'S BEST ROASTED SALSA

An easy throw-together salsa that will have every chip in town coming your way. The deep roasted flavor and simple ingredients will make this your new go-to dipper. The amazing flavor comes from the variety of hot peppers used in combination with the fire-roasted tomatoes and tang of the vinegar and lime juice.

1 (28-oz [794-g]) can fire-roasted tomatoes

½ cup (20 g) chopped fresh cilantro

½ cup (25 g) chopped green onions

3 medium-size cloves garlic

2 tsp (10 g) sea salt

2 tsp (10 ml) fresh lime juice

1 tsp apple cider vinegar

1 tsp crushed red pepper (see notes)

¼ to ½ tsp chipotle powder (see notes)

¼ to ½ tsp cayenne pepper (see notes)

Put the tomatoes, cilantro, green onions, garlic, salt, lime juice, vinegar, crushed red pepper, chipotle powder and cayenne pepper into a food processor and blend until puréed.

Notes: This sauce is best if made ahead of time and the flavors are allowed to marinate.

Adjust the amount of seasonings to get the spice level you want.

SMOKY TANGY CREAM

A touch of smoke and tang and a lot of cream makes this the perfect sauce to up the ante on any meal. This one was a favorite among the recipe testers because of its unique ability to capture such a wide variety of flavors. Your taste buds move along the range of sweet, spicy, tangy and smoky in perfect sequence. Don't say I didn't warn you if you eat it with a spoon.

1 cup (112 g) raw cashews (see note)

1 cup (240 ml) water

3 tbsp (29 g) chopped red onion

2 tbsp (30 ml) fresh lemon juice

2 medium-size cloves garlic

1½ tsp (4 g) smoked paprika

1 tsp sea salt

⅛ to ¼ tsp chipotle seasoning, to taste

Put the cashews, water, red onion, lemon juice, garlic, paprika, salt and chipotle seasoning into a high-speed blender and purée until smooth. Refrigerate the cream to thicken.

Note: If you are not using a high-speed blender, there are a couple of options for making your sauce smooth: You can use a coffee grinder to grind everything to a fine powder, or make sure to soak your cashews overnight, or for at least 2 to 3 hours. If you forget, you can also boil them for 30 minutes.

Yield: 1½ CUPS
(355 ML)

level: 1

LOW-FAT CREAMY CURRY SAUCE

The perfect sauce for beginner curry-ers. The added sweet potato helps cut the fat and gives an extra layer of sweetness. Adjust the curry spice to reach the fragrant and spicy depth you prefer, and dig in!

1 cup (240 ml) light coconut milk

½ cup (100 g) cooked sweet potato (see notes)

1 tbsp (15 ml) tamari or soy sauce

1 tbsp (15 ml) fresh lime juice

2 tsp (10 ml) maple syrup

2 cloves garlic

1 to 2 tsp (2 to 4 g) curry powder, to taste

¼ to ½ tsp sea salt (see notes)

1 tbsp (3 g) fresh cilantro

½ to 1 tsp red pepper flakes (for extra spice)

Put the coconut milk, sweet potato, tamari, lime juice, maple syrup, garlic, curry powder and salt into a high-speed blender and purée until smooth. Add the cilantro and red pepper flakes and pulse until well chopped and incorporated. Refrigerate the sauce to thicken.

Notes: Cook the potato in the microwave or oven. I don't recommend boiling it because it makes the potato too wet.

You may need more or less salt depending on whether you use reduced-sodium or regular tamari or soy sauce.

TARTAR SAUCE EXTREME

Not your traditional tartar sauce . . . but way better. All the zing of the original but made with all whole foods so there's none of the unhealthy ingredients. You'll be able to drizzle, dip or dunk without any regret! It's amazing any way you use it. I suggest piling it on high!

1½ cups (167 g) raw cashews (see note)

1 cup (240 ml) water

2 tsp (10 ml) distilled white vinegar

1 to 3 tsp (5 to 15 ml) fresh lemon juice, to taste

1 medium-size clove garlic

1 tsp sea salt

⅛ tsp ground mustard seed

⅛ tsp ground black pepper

½ cup (90 g) chopped dill pickles

¼ cup (25 g) capers

2 tbsp (5 g) chopped parsley

Hot sauce to taste, optional but highly recommended

Put the cashews, water, vinegar, lemon juice, garlic, salt, mustard seed and black pepper into a high-speed blender and purée until smooth. Then add the pickles, capers, parsley and hot sauce, if using, and pulse until chopped but still chunky. Refrigerate the sauce to thicken.

Note: If you are not using a high-speed blender, there are a couple of options for making your sauce smooth: You can use a coffee grinder to grind everything to a fine powder, or make sure to soak your cashews overnight, or for at least 2 to 3 hours. If you forget, you can also boil them for 30 minutes.

ULTIMATE ONION DIP

Featuring whole foods and dairy-free, this onion dip just became healthy, so grab those potato chips (well, I guess kinda healthy). You can put it on everything from burgers to sandwiches to your spoon. This is the prefect dip for watching the game or just whenever the mood strikes. Obsession is at a high over here.

1¼ cups (139 g) raw cashews (see note)

1 cup (240 ml) water

2 tbsp (30 ml) distilled white vinegar

2 tsp (10 ml) fresh lemon juice

¼ tsp ground mustard seed

3 tbsp (38 g) minced onion flakes

2¼ tsp (8 g) onion powder

1½ tsp (1 g) dried parsley

¾ tsp garlic

¾ tsp sea salt

¼ tsp celery seed

Put the cashews, water, vinegar, lemon juice and mustard seed into a high-speed blender and purée until smooth. Add the onion flakes, onion powder, parsley, garlic, salt and celery seed and pulse until mixed well. Refrigerate the dip to thicken.

Note: If you are not using a high-speed blender, there are a couple of options for making your sauce smooth: You can use a coffee grinder to grind everything to a fine powder, or make sure to soak your cashews overnight, or for at least 2 to 3 hours. If you forget, you can also boil them for 30 minutes.

SKINNY PEANUT SAUCE

You can now enjoy peanut sauce without all the guilt. Run for your blenders! Beans replace some of the peanut butter to give this sauce a creamy twist and lower the fat. So full of flavor you'll never miss it!

1 cup (200 g) cooked or canned white beans (such as great northern beans), drained and rinsed

¼ cup (60 ml) tamari or soy sauce

3 tbsp (34 g) creamy peanut butter

3 tbsp (45 ml) rice vinegar

3 tbsp (45 ml) maple syrup

1 tbsp (15 ml) fresh lime juice

2 medium-size cloves garlic

½ tsp ground ginger

½ to 1 tsp crushed red pepper, optional

½ tsp sea salt, optional (see notes)

Extra water to thin out, optional (see notes), add 1 tbsp (15 ml) at a time

Put the beans, tamari, peanut butter, vinegar, maple syrup, lime juice, garlic, ginger, red pepper, if using, and salt into a high-speed blender, and purée until smooth. Refrigerate the sauce to thicken.

Notes: You may need some salt depending on whether you use reduced-sodium or regular tamari or soy sauce.

This is a thin sauce, so add the water only if you want it to border the consistency of a dressing.

THE VEGAN SOUR CREAM

I lost count of how many trials this vegan sour cream took. From research on flavors that help counteract the sweetness in cashews, to multiple trials and errors, I finally landed on this perfect recipe. All whole food ingredients for a flavor that is so close to the real thing. It doesn't get much better than this!

1¼ cups (139 g) raw cashews (see notes)

1 cup (240 ml) water (see notes)

8½ tsp (42 ml) distilled white vinegar

1½ tsp (7 ml) fresh lemon juice

¼ tsp ground mustard seed

⅛ tsp freshly chopped garlic

Put the cashews, water, vinegar, lemon juice, mustard seed and garlic into a high-speed blender and purée until smooth. Refrigerate the sour cream to thicken.

Notes: If you are not using a high-speed blender, there are a couple of options for making your sauce smooth: You can use a coffee grinder to grind everything to a fine powder, or make sure to soak your cashews overnight, or for at least 2 to 3 hours. If you forget, you can also boil them for 30 minutes.

Feel free to add less water if you want a thicker sour cream, but keep in mind you will lose some of that neutral flavor I have achieved.

HEALTHY VEGAN MAYO, WHAT?

Finally, a whole food–based, oil-free mayo you will love! Unlike the traditional variety, this mayonnaise is actually heart-healthy. So slather it on without guilt or worry!

1½ cups (167 g) raw cashews (see note)

¾ cup plus 1 tbsp (192 ml) water

2 tbsp (30 ml) distilled white vinegar

2 tsp (10 ml) fresh lemon juice

¾ tsp sea salt

⅛ tsp ground mustard seed

⅛ tsp freshly chopped garlic

Put the cashews, water, vinegar, lemon juice, salt, mustard seed and garlic into a high-speed blender and purée until smooth. Refrigerate the mayo to thicken.

Note: If you are not using a high-speed blender, there are a couple of options for making your sauce smooth: You can use a coffee grinder to grind everything to a fine powder, or make sure to soak your cashews overnight, or for at least 2 to 3 hours. If you forget, you can also boil them for 30 minutes.

ALL-AMERICAN SPECIAL SAUCE

The perfect complement to an all-American burger, this special sauce has all the flavor of the traditional version but none of the bad ingredients. Made of all whole foods, it's actually healthy, so you can love it without worry. Like a fine wine, this sauce gets better as it ages; make it ahead of time so it can marinate for the ultimate flavor bomb. Tangy, sweet and salty all rolled into one.

1½ cups (167 g) raw cashews (see note)

1 cup (240 ml) water

1 tbsp (15 ml) apple cider vinegar

4 tsp (20 g) tomato paste

4 tsp (20 ml) fresh lemon juice

1 tbsp (15 ml) yellow mustard

1 tsp onion powder

1 tsp sea salt

1 medium-size clove garlic

¼ cup (25 g) sweet pickle relish

Put the cashews, water, vinegar, tomato paste, lemon juice, mustard, onion powder, salt and garlic into a blender and purée until smooth. Add the relish and pulse to incorporate. Refrigerate the mixture to thicken.

Note: If you are not using a high-speed blender, there are a couple of options for making your sauce smooth: You can use a coffee grinder to grind everything to a fine powder, or make sure to soak your cashews overnight, or for at least 2 to 3 hours. If you forget, you can also boil them for 30 minutes.

CREAMY DILL WITH A TANGY TWIST

This velvety smooth and creamy dill sauce is heaven for all dill fans. With amazing flavor and a texture to die for, this sauce is one that you're always going to want to have on hand. I may have been caught eating it soup-style.

1¼ cups (140 g) raw cashews (see note)

1 cup (240 ml) unsweetened plain cashew or almond milk

¾ cup (151 g) cooked or canned white beans (such as great northern beans), drained and rinsed

3 tbsp (45 ml) fresh lemon juice

3 tbsp (45 ml) apple cider vinegar

1 medium-size clove garlic

1 tsp salt

½ cup (20 g) fresh dill

Put the cashews, milk, beans, lemon juice, vinegar, garlic and salt into a high-speed blender and purée until smooth. Add the dill, and pulse until chopped and well mixed. Refrigerate the sauce to thicken.

You can also add some of the dill with the first ingredients to give the sauce a nice light-green color and more intense dill flavor since it will be puréed in if you do so. Then add the remainder and pulse to get some whole dill pieces.

Note: If you are not using a high-speed blender, there are a couple of options for making your sauce smooth: You can use a coffee grinder to grind everything to a fine powder, or make sure to soak your cashews overnight, or for at least 2 to 3 hours. If you forget, you can also boil them for 30 minutes.

QUICK-AND-EASY PIZZA SAUCE

The easiest pizza sauce you will ever make. So versatile, perfect to have on hand and so much better than the jarred stuff. Keep it in your fridge for up to a week for a quick grab-and-go option.

1 cup (230 g) tomato paste

½ cup (118 ml) low-sodium veggie broth (see notes)

1 tbsp (2 g) dried thyme

1 tbsp (2 g) dried basil

2 tsp (1 g) dried oregano

1 tsp garlic powder

1 tsp sea salt

1 tsp maple syrup

½ to 1 tsp crushed red pepper, optional (see notes)

¼ tsp ground black pepper

Put the tomato paste, broth, thyme, basil, oregano, garlic powder, salt, maple syrup, crushed red pepper and black pepper in a bowl and mix well.

Notes: This sauce is best if made ahead of time and the flavors are allowed to marinate. This also helps the dried herbs to soften and allows the spices to fully combine with the tomato paste. If your sauce seems a little "gritty," then allow it to sit longer. You can speed this up by heating it slightly.

You can use water instead of broth, but the broth adds great flavor. Add more or less broth for the consistency you like.

Add more or less crushed red pepper to achieve the level of spice you prefer, or leave it out altogether.

NO-COOK ENCHILADA SAUCE

An easy-to-throw-together sauce that requires no cooking! Just whisk together and you're ready to rumble. This sauce is the perfect consistency for a burger, or thin it out a bit to use as a true enchilada sauce. Any way you use it, it's amazing!

1 cup (230 g) tomato paste

1 cup (240 ml) low-sodium veggie broth (see notes)

5 tsp (25 ml) maple syrup

1 tbsp (8 g) smoked paprika

1½ tsp (4 g) chili powder (see notes)

1½ tsp (4 g) cumin

1½ tsp (4 g) onion powder

1½ tsp (4 g) garlic powder

1½ tsp (4 g) sea salt

1 tsp apple cider vinegar

Put the tomato paste, broth, maple syrup, paprika, chili powder, cumin, onion powder, garlic powder, salt and vinegar in a bowl and mix well with a whisk until smooth. Warm the sauce in the microwave or on the stovetop when you're ready to serve it, but warming is not necessary.

Notes: This sauce is best if made ahead of time and the flavors are allowed to marinate. This also allows the spices to fully combine with the tomato paste. If your sauce seems a little "gritty," then allow it to sit longer. You can speed this up by heating it slightly.

You can use water instead of broth, but the broth adds great flavor. Keep in mind that this is a thick enchilada sauce, so you can add more or less broth for the consistency you like.

Decrease the amount of chili powder if you are sensitive to spice.

EASY HOMEMADE BBQ SAUCE

Whip up this homemade sauce in no time. It's way better than the bottled version and much healthier. You can even add more sweet or tang to meet your BBQ sauce desires. My newfound favorite snack is dipping fresh, crisp fries into this sauce. Get out a bowl and pile it on, cowboy!

1 cup (230 g) tomato paste

½ cup (118 ml) low-sodium veggie broth (see notes)

3 tbsp (45 ml) maple syrup

3 tbsp (45 ml) molasses

4 tsp (20 ml) apple cider vinegar

2½ tsp (12 ml) liquid smoke

2 tsp (5 g) chili powder

1½ tsp (8 g) sea salt

1 tsp garlic powder

Put the tomato paste, broth, maple syrup, molasses, vinegar, liquid smoke, chili powder, salt and garlic powder in a bowl and mix well until smooth.

People have many different opinions when it comes to the kind of BBQ sauce they like. If you fall in the spicy camp, then add more chili powder ¼ teaspoon at a time to get the level of spice you like. If you are in the sweet camp, add more maple syrup ½ teaspoon at a time until you get the sweetness you like. But if you are in the tangy camp, add more vinegar ¼ teaspoon at a time until you get the tang you like. This is a good middle-of-the road BBQ sauce, the perfect average mix of sweet, spicy and tangy, according to what I like and the opinions of those who've tried it.

Notes: You can use water instead of broth, but I find the broth gives it a bit more flavor. Add more or less broth for the thickness you like.

This sauce is best if made ahead of time so the flavors are allowed to marinate. Marinating also allows the spices to fully combine with the tomato paste. If your sauce seems a little "gritty," then allow it to sit longer. You can speed this up by heating it slightly.

CREAM SAUCE FOR THE SOUL

Yield: 2 TO 2½ CUPS (473 TO 591 ML)

Level: 1

You will never miss the dairy after you've tried this creamy heaven. A touch of tang and a hint of white wine make this the ultimate in creamy comfort. Adjust the garlic to meet your preferred level of garlic breath!

¾ cup (151 g) cooked potato (see notes)

¾ cup (177 ml) unsweetened plain cashew or almond milk

½ cup (56 g) raw cashews (see notes)

¼ to ½ cup (60 to 118 ml) veggie broth (see notes)

1 tbsp (15 ml) white or cooking wine (see notes)

2 tsp (10 ml) apple cider vinegar

2 tsp (10 ml) fresh lemon juice

1 small- or medium-size clove garlic, to taste

¾ tsp sea salt

Put the potato, milk, cashews, broth, wine, vinegar, lemon juice, garlic and salt into a high-speed blender and purée until smooth. Refrigerate the sauce to thicken.

Notes: Cook the potato in the microwave or oven. I don't recommend boiling it because it makes the potato too wet.

If you are not using a high-speed blender, there are a couple of options for making your sauce smooth: You can use a coffee grinder to grind everything to a fine powder, or make sure to soak your cashews overnight, or for at least 2 to 3 hours. If you forget, you can also boil them for 30 minutes.

You can easily substitute water for the broth, however the broth gives it a nicer flavor.

Wine is highly recommended for ultimate flavor, but if you don't want to use wine, feel free to replace it with more broth. Adjust the amount of broth depending on how thick you want the sauce.

YIAYIA'S AUTHENTIC TZATZIKI

From a village in Greece to your table, this family favorite tzatziki recipe is now dairy-free! I have the green light from Greeks themselves for this one, so dig in knowing you're not compromising authenticity!

1½ cups (270 g) peeled and grated cucumber

1½ cups (167 g) raw cashews (see note)

1¼ cups (295 ml) water

2 tbsp (30 ml) fresh lemon juice

1 tbsp (15 ml) distilled white vinegar

4 medium-size cloves garlic

¾ tsp sea salt

¼ tsp ground black pepper

2 tbsp (5 g) fresh dill

Put the grated cucumber in a paper towel, wrap and squeeze out the excess water.

Put all of the cashews, water, lemon juice, vinegar, garlic, salt and pepper into a high-speed blender and purée until smooth. Add the cucumber and blend until well incorporated. Add the dill and pulse until chopped and well mixed. Refrigerate the tzatziki to thicken.

Note: If you are not using a high-speed blender, there are a couple of options for making your sauce smooth: You can use a coffee grinder to grind everything to a fine powder, or make sure to soak your cashews overnight, or for at least 2 to 3 hours. If you forget, you can also boil them for 30 minutes.

STOVETOP TASTY TERIYAKI SAUCE

Way better than a store-bought bottle, this teriyaki is quick to put together and perfect to drizzle on anything and everything. Watch it closely so it doesn't burn; I won't tell you how many times I've learned this lesson.

½ cup plus 2 tbsp (148 ml) maple syrup

½ cup (118 ml) tamari or soy sauce

¼ cup (60 ml) water

2 tbsp (30 ml) mirin (see notes)

1 tbsp (6 g) brown rice flour (see notes)

1½ tsp (4 g) garlic powder

Put the maple syrup, tamari, water, mirin, brown rice, flour and garlic powder into a pot and whisk well. Heat it over medium-high until the liquid begins to boil. Reduce the heat to medium and cook until thick, stirring frequently, about 5 to 7 minutes. Don't overcook as the sauce thickens more upon cooling.

Notes: Mirin can be found in the Asian section of your supermarket.

You can use cornstarch instead of brown rice flour if you don't have it.

MIND-BLOWING CHOCOLATE SAUCE

This chocolate sauce is unlike any other. Tomato paste gives an amazing tang while the espresso deepens the chocolate flavor. Drizzle it on everything or eat it with a spoon. Don't knock it until you try it!

1½ cups (270 g) vegan chocolate chips

6 tbsp (88 ml) unsweetened plain cashew or almond milk (see note)

1½ tsp (7 g) tomato paste

½ tsp finely ground espresso beans

½ tsp vanilla extract

¼ sea salt

Combine the chocolate chips, milk, tomato paste, espresso, vanilla extract and salt in a bowl or pot. Microwave for 30 seconds or heat on the stovetop until the chocolate chips are melted and the sauce is warm, about 4 to 5 minutes. Whisk well until smooth.

Note: Add more or less milk to get the thickness you prefer. Store the sauce in the fridge and warm it up before serving it to get the smooth, drippy texture back.

STICKY ALMOND CARAMEL

A twist on your traditional caramel sauce. No heavy cream needed to get this amazing flavor—just heat a few ingredients, whisk well and voilà! Caramel sauce for your sweet tooth. This can be used in place of caramel for anything and everything: think poured over ice cream, drizzled over waffles or pancakes, or even mixed into yogurt!

¾ cup (177 ml) maple syrup

½ cup (90 g) almond butter

1 tsp vanilla extract

¼ tsp sea salt

Combine the maple syrup, almond butter, vanilla extract and salt in a bowl or pot. Microwave it at 30 second increments until melted and warm, or heat it on the stovetop over medium-low heat, mixing constantly so it doesn't burn, about 4 to 5 minutes. Whisk well until smooth.

Sides

Sometimes I feel like getting fancy. Maybe it's the days when I don't have #1 (aka Mike Tyson) snuggling against my back all night, or maybe it's the two hours without constant fights over why the baby is hoarding all the blue cars, but either way the boost of energy gets me excited to throw in a little something extra with our dinner.

These sides are simple to make and can be served with any of the recipes in this book. The only warning I give is make sure to place the cooling sheet out of reach. And by *reach,* I mean *yours.* There may or may not have been a few instances when I had to "pretend" the batch burned and only a few lone survivors were left for dinner.

TATERS AND HERBS

Just some good old fries with an added punch of flavor from the combination of fresh herbs and dried seasonings. These are perfect as a side or even stuffed in your favorite burger or burrito!

2 medium-size russet or red potatoes (about 5½ inches [14 cm] long)

2 tsp (10 g) sea salt, divided

2 tbsp (30 ml) liquid from a can of chickpeas, or drizzle of oil (see note)

¼ cup (10 g) finely chopped cilantro

2 tsp (5 g) onion powder

2 tsp (5 g) dried parsley

Preheat the oven to 450°F (232°C).

Peel the potatoes and slice them into french fry–size slices, trying to keep the pieces as uniform as possible. Place them in a water bath and allow them to soak for 5 to 10 minutes to remove some of the starch while you gather the rest of the ingredients. Rinse the potatoes and when the water runs clear, place them in a colander.

Sprinkle half of the salt over the potatoes and mix well to incorporate. Allow them to sit for 5 to 10 minutes for the salt to bring out some of the water in the potatoes.

Place the potatoes on a towel and rub them well to dry, wiping off the salt. Place them in a bowl.

Pour the chickpea liquid over the potatoes and mix well to coat. Drain the excess liquid.

Put the rest of the salt, the cilantro, onion powder and parsley into the bowl and mix well to coat the potatoes evenly. Spread them onto a parchment-lined cookie sheet, making sure that the pieces don't touch. This allows each fry to get crispy on all sides.

Bake for 20 to 30 minutes, depending on the thickness. Check at 20 minutes, mix up the fries to expose new sides, and continue to bake them until they're crispy.

Note: The liquid from the can of chickpeas is also known as aquafaba. It helps coat things so that the dry ingredients will stick better and gives them a nice crisp when baked. I reserve it and freeze it in ice cube trays for future use. If you are okay with oil, then you can substitute the bean liquid for a drizzle of your favorite oil.

SMOKY SEASONED SWEET POTATO FRIES

The sweetness of sweet potatoes and hint of smoke make these fries some of the tastiest I've ever had. They're perfect straight from the oven with their slightly crispy exterior. You better make it a double because once you've started eating them you won't be able to stop. And then your family is going to be mad . . . don't ask me how I know.

2 medium-size sweet potatoes

2 tbsp (30 ml) liquid from a can of chickpeas, or drizzle of oil (see note)

2 tsp (10 g) sea salt

2 tsp (5 g) smoked paprika

2 tsp (5 g) garlic powder

2 tsp (5 g) onion powder

4 tsp (5 g) bread crumbs (gluten-free if needed)

Preheat the oven to 450°F (232°C).

Peel the potatoes and slice them into french fry–size slices, trying to keep the pieces as uniform as possible. Place them in a bowl.

Pour the chickpea liquid over the potatoes and mix well to coat. Drain the excess liquid.

Put the salt, paprika, garlic powder, onion powder and bread crumbs into the bowl and mix well to coat the potatoes evenly. Spread them onto a parchment-lined cookie sheet, making sure that the pieces don't touch. This allows each fry to get crispy on all sides.

Bake for 20 to 30 minutes, depending on the thickness. Check at 20 minutes, mix up the fries to expose new sides, and continue to bake them until they're crispy.

Note: The liquid from the can of chickpeas is also known as aquafaba. It helps coat things so that the dry ingredients will stick better and gives them a nice crisp when baked. I reserve it and freeze it in ice cube trays for future use. If you are okay with oil, then you can substitute the bean liquid for a drizzle of your favorite oil.

CRISPY ZUCCHINI CHIPS

Trying to get your kids to eat some extra veggies? These crispy masked goodies are the perfect way. If you call them straight up chips, they may not ask questions. I tend to get creative with my moody middle.

2 large zucchini

BATTER

2 cups (193 g) almond flour (see notes)

2 cups (480 ml) unsweetened plain cashew or almond milk

CRISPY COATING

1 cup (170 g) cornmeal

½ cup (50 g) almond flour (see notes)

½ cup (30 g) bread crumbs (gluten-free if needed)

3 tsp (15 g) sea salt

4 tsp (2 g) dried thyme

4 tsp (2 g) dried rosemary

4 tsp (10 g) garlic powder

Preheat the oven to 450°F (232°C).

Cut the zucchini into round slices about ⅛ inch (3 mm) thick.

Make the zucchini batter by whisking the almond flour and milk in a bowl until a thick batter forms.

To make the crispy coating, mix the cornmeal, almond flour, bread crumbs, salt, thyme, rosemary and garlic powder in a shallow baking dish.

Using one hand for the batter and one for breading (this helps avoid clumping of the breading), dip each zucchini piece in the batter, then place in the breading dish and cover with crispy coating. Place each piece on a parchment-lined cookie sheet.

Bake for 15 minutes. Flip them over and bake for 5 to 7 minutes until brown and crispy.

Notes: I use a fine-ground blanched almond flour, but because this isn't a baked good, any almond flour would work.

There will be plenty of crispy coating left, but I want a lot so the coating won't get too clumpy and sticky at the end and so every chip has an equal chance to be coated well.

CURRIED CARROT FRIES

If you're looking for the perfect match to your curry-flavored dinner, this is it. Not your traditional fry, but a great way to get in a few extra veggies! The lime, cilantro and curry flavors are a great combo with the sweetness a carrot brings. A match made in heaven!

6 large carrots

1 tbsp (15 ml) liquid from a can of chickpeas, or drizzle of oil (see note)

1 tbsp (15 ml) fresh lime juice

1 tsp sea salt

¼ cup (10 g) finely chopped cilantro

2 to 4 tsp (5 to 10 g) curry seasoning, to taste

2 tsp (5 g) garlic powder

Preheat the oven to 450°F (232°C).

Peel the carrots and slice them into french fry–size slices, trying to keep the pieces as uniform as possible. Place them in a bowl.

Pour the chickpea liquid and lime juice over the carrots and mix well to coat them. Drain the excess liquid.

Put the salt, cilantro, curry seasoning and garlic powder into the bowl and mix well to coat the carrots evenly. Spread them onto a parchment-lined cookie sheet, making sure that the pieces don't touch. This allows each fry to get crispy on all sides.

Bake for 20 to 30 minutes, depending on the thickness. Check at 20 minutes, mix up the fries to expose new sides and continue to bake them until they're crispy.

Note: The liquid from the can of chickpeas is also known as aquafaba. It helps coat things so that the dry ingredients will stick better and gives them a nice crisp when baked. I reserve it and freeze it in ice cube trays for future use. If you are okay with oil, then you can substitute the bean liquid with a drizzle of your favorite oil.

Help! I Screwed It Up
(AND OTHER RESOURCES)

There are many reasons that things can turn out differently; we are human, after all. I tested and trialed these recipes many times, as well as had others try them out for me. It's through these trials and errors that I came up with this list of possible reasons why your results may be a bit different.

- **Measuring your fresh herbs and chopped greens.** When measuring fresh herbs and greens, I always chop before I measure. If you don't, you may have a different amount in the end since you can fit more chopped herbs into a measuring utensil. When in doubt, measure packed.

- **Overall measuring.** In order to get a true exact measurement, you need to run a flat edge over the top of your measuring tool. You won't believe how easy it is to get a little bit extra of each ingredient. A little bit here and a little bit there can add up to a small change in your end result.

- **Pulsing.** Over- or underpulsing a mixture with beans can yield a mushier end texture or even a mixture that won't stick together. It takes practice to get that perfect consistency, but a rule of thumb is to use the pulse button, stop and check the underneath portion of the mixture, and if it still doesn't stick together when sampling, pulse a few more times until it does.

- **Instructions.** Make sure to follow each instruction carefully. Read ahead and be prepared with what you need so you'll be ready for the next step. I can't tell you how many times I've had to quickly wash and chop something.

- **Substituting.** I have written each recipe with the ingredients we use every day. Any substitutions can affect the end result. For example, if you use long-grain or basmati rice instead of short-grain rice, you won't get a burger mixture that stays together as well, since short-grain rice has more starch and will get stickier. The only substitutions that will usually end up okay are if you prefer to use a ready-made sauce, such as jarred pizza sauce or bottled ranch. I'm not going to lie: my homemade versions are tastier, but I totally get the need to shave off a little extra time. Sometimes even 5 minutes make all the difference to sanity.

- **Be careful of stragglers.** When cooking, rinsing, etc., make sure that you put in only what the recipe calls for and drain any extra juices or water. It's easy to dump sautéed veggies into a bowl and not notice the small trail of juice that follows them. This small bit can give your recipe extra moistness it doesn't need and alter your end result.

FEEDING MY FAMILY AND TRYING TO STAY SANE

Let me emphasize the word *trying.* Life with kids is a bit unpredictable. One minute they are happily playing; the next they are flopped on the floor because they caught a glimpse of the brown beans you put in the burger, and they've decided they only eat black. Staying on top of your game is the key to success, and I'm here to share my tricks.

- Keep cooked (I use canned) beans on hand at all times. If you're fancy enough to cook your own, make batches and keep them in the fridge, or even in the freezer, if you don't expect to use them within the week.

- Have cooked rice or quinoa on hand. I love the frozen brown rice in a box. It warms up with perfect consistency. There are a few recipes that include cooking directions for the rice because they require cooking with certain flavors or spices. However, many recipes can be made very quickly if you have precooked rice ready.

- Look ahead at what you are making and prechop or preslice everything you need. It's the prep that takes longer than the actual recipe most of the time. I sometimes even premix all the spices into one container and then I can easily throw them in when I need them. Make the sauce early. Sauces only get better with time, so giving them a day ahead to marinate yields the best flavor.

- Double the recipe. I love to make extra of everything and freeze the leftovers. Having ready-to-go burgers in the freezer is a lifesaver. For real, it's my savior on those crazy nights when cereal is the only other option. Not that we don't sometimes have cereal. Or ice cream. Or chips and salsa. We are human, after all.

Acknowledgments

This book was definitely not a single-handed accomplishment. It was a true collaboration of everyone around me who allowed me to accomplish this crazy dream of mine. I had an amazing group of recipe testers who jumped at the chance to give me feedback, and for that I am eternally grateful. I was blessed with an amazing editor and publisher who were patient with my millions of questions and my OCD tendencies to make everything as perfect as I could.

An enormous dose of respect and appreciation goes to my friend and family photographer Chris Nelson, of Chris Nelson Photography, for capturing my crazy little family in the absolute perfect way. I am humbled and blessed to have worked with her for the lifestyle photos in this book.

Thank you to my friends, who are still there for me even though I had to take a step back from wine nights, play dates and fun outings while I dove headfirst into this project.

Thank you to my mom for bringing dinners on Tuesdays, for being here to help wrangle my monsters so I could focus on one thing for once and for the endless help of testing the recipes I second-guessed myself on.

Thanks to my sister, who let me half pay attention to family life these past few months without giving me grief.

Thank you to my nanny for being there to play with my kids when I had to take a step back to write this book.

Thank you to my kids for dealing with "work mommy" and trying everything I made, even if they had eaten burgers and burritos for months at a time.

But most of all, thank you to my husband for allowing me to come at him with a spoon even after he had brushed his teeth. I love you all to the moon and back and could never have done this without you. They say it takes a village, and this certainly does apply to writing a cookbook.

About the Author

Sophia DeSantis is the founder of Veggies Don't Bite, a plant-based food blog that shows how leaving out animal products, gluten and (refined) sugar does not mean leaving out delicious flavor. She believes that she simply creates good food that just happens to be vegan. She welcomes all types of eaters so they can see how longtime favorite foods can still be enjoyed in a healthy, wholesome, whole food, plant-based way.

Sophia has been featured on many websites, including Foodgawker, Finding Vegan, BuzzFeed, Huffington Post and Red Tricycle, to name a few, and has written guest posts for a variety of other sites and features in multiple print magazines. Through her website, www.veggiesdontbite.com, she hopes to reach people interested in making a positive health change in their lives. She loves working with families, especially those with children, because establishing healthy choices early in life will lead to a lifetime of good habits.

She lives in San Diego, where she tames three young boys and one husband, and lives life to the fullest every day. Her motto is eat, play, relax, repeat.

Index